ADVANCE PRAISE FOR
the RULES

The Rules is an excellent and practical guide to being truly human. It's about the freedom to love God and neighbor, as a love response to Jesus, who so freely loved us. What could be better than that?

—CHARLIE PEACOCK
Musician, author, and director of the Art House

When I hear "Ten Commandments," I immediately think of Charlton Heston with a beard and Yul Brynner in a skirt, so obviously the importance of these ten instructions has wavered at some point in my life. It is refreshing and convicting to have these rules brought back to the forefront of my mind—to remember why my morals are in place and why they are there to begin with; to bring glory to God.

—NATHAN COCHRAN
Mercy Me

This is gives us great insight to "the rules" and paints a clear picture as to how to live by them. *The Rules* become a freedom worth fighting for, as opposed to "unattainable chores," in our pursuit of Christ.

DAVID TOSTI
PAX217

Mark Nicholas takes the Ten Commandments and breaks them down to show specific ways God's rules are the ultimate freedom. It is a new look at the old laws that govern our lives as Christians.

JILL PHILLIPS
Singer/songwriter

Just such a fresh perspective on how God wants us to live couldn't be more timely for our world. Today's youth and young adults will find Mark's work especially crucial to their foundations as they walk in these uncertain times. *The Rules* takes the broad-based principles of our God, and speaks to specifics in the lives of us all. This is a truly relevant work.

RIC "FORM" ROBBINS
GRITS' DJ and Producer

the
RULES

TEN TO LIVE BY

MARK NICHOLAS

TRANSIT
www.TransitBooks.com

The Rules: Ten to Live By

Copyright © 2003 by Mark Nicholas

Published by W Publishing Group, a Division of Thomas Nelson, Inc., P.O. Box 141000, Nashville, Tennessee 37214.

Senior Editor: Kate Etue
Editiorial Staff: Lauren Weller, Valerie Gibbs, Deborah Wiseman, and Lori Jones
Cover Design: Matt Lehman at Anderson Thomas Design, Nashville, TN
Page Design: Book & Graphic Design, Nashville, TN

Unless otherwise noted, Scripture quotations used in this book are from The Holy Bible, New Century Version (NCV), copyright © 1987, 1988, 1991 by Word Publishing, a Division of Thomas Nelson, Inc. Used by permission. Scripture quotations noted NKJV are from The New King James Version, copyright 1979, 1980, 1982, Thomas Nelson, Inc.

Library of Congress Cataloging-in-Publication Data
Nicholas, Mark, 1970–
    The rules : ten to live by / by Mark Nicholas.
        p. cm.
    ISBN 0-8499-4417-1
    1. Ten commandments. 2. Christian teenagers—Religious life. I. Title.
    BV4655.N47 2003
    241.5'2--dc21

2003002433

Printed and bound in the United States of America

04 05 06 07 PHX 7 6

CONTENTS

FOREWORD

Following the laws of God is not a matter of *making* Him the Lord of your life. His Lordship is already an indisputable fact, because He is God. The Ten Commandments is not a list of things Jesus wants us to do or things withheld from us to make sure that we do not have fun. The gift of the law is in actuality a way by which we can fully receive the limitless love the Lord of the universe already feels for us.

Jesus, your Creator, knows you more intimately than any person ever could and loves you more deeply than you can fathom. It is impossible for Him to give you the rules described in this book as anything other than personal instructions about how to fully accept, return and share His love, the very reason you exist.

I pray that reading this book will do more than just expound upon the "no-no's" you have probably heard over and over in your life. Search deeper, beyond your self-control and outside behavior into your heart and motivation so that obeying the Ten Commandments can be an honest response of love to a God whose joy and delight comes from being close to you.

MARK STUART

INTRODUCTION

Do you ever feel like you live your life on the brink of being out of control? Are your days so hectic that you don't seem to have time to stop and consider what are right or wrong choices? How often do you feel confused about the issues of love, money, war, crime, spirituality, or God? Do you have big plans for your life or none at all? Do you ever wonder what the purpose of your life is anyway? If this sounds like you, you're not alone. In fact, I would venture to say that every single person has wrestled with these thoughts and questions at some point.

Life is not always easy. Some days it is simply a glorious thing just to be alive, and other days we wish we had never even gotten out of bed. Thankfully, God is looking out for us. He cares for both our good and our bad days. He desires to help us walk through confusing or difficult situations. And He has given us His Word. Through the course of this book, we'll explore issues of morality, meaning, failure, glory, and freedom as revealed through the Bible with the Ten Commandments.

Let's take a quick look at why our lives seem to have so many twists and turns. To do this we'll need to go back to the beginning, to the biblical story of the first man and woman, Adam and Eve. You've probably heard their story many times, but it's worth looking at once again, because it affects the whole rest of history, including you and me.

Many years ago, God created all that exists, including light, dark, water, earth, sky, plants, and animals. God also made a man and a woman, named Adam and Eve, with a distinct purpose and place above the rest of creation. These humans were created in God's image and were instructed to rule the creatures of the earth and tend to the garden in Eden. Have you ever heard that phrase "created in God's image" and wondered what that means? It means that God gave them many characteristics that are like His. Like God, the humans had souls, authority over land and animals, and the ability to think, reason, be creative, have relationships, and do good.[1]

Adam and Eve were free to enjoy each other and God's created earth for eternity, with only one rule. God told them not to eat from the Tree of the Knowledge of Good and Evil or they would die. Choosing not to trust in God's warning and provision, but rather to listen to the tempting words of the serpent, Adam and Eve ate fruit from the forbidden tree. This disobedience was the first instance of human sin in the world, causing a break from the original intent for life on earth for the rest of humanity. It is also interesting to note, however, that immediately after this rupture, God began to show the humans mercy and foreshadow the salvation of mankind.[2] For example, God made them clothes to cover themselves, since Adam and Eve were now aware and ashamed of their nakedness. He also placed a guard in front of the Tree of Life, which would have locked them into sin and suffering for eternity, had Adam and Eve eaten of it. And most importantly God said to the serpent, "One of her [Eve's] descendants will crush your head" (Genesis 3:15), alluding to an ultimate victory over sin and death to be brought about by Jesus Christ.

Looking at that story, we see perfection, followed by the beginnings of a broken world, along with a glimpse of where the future is heading. We'll look through this framework as we examine the world we're living in today.

Now what does all of this have to do with the Ten Commandments? In the following chapters we'll explore how

---

1. (New Geneva Study Bible, p. 9 notes).
2. (New Geneva Study Bible, p. 13 notes).

God gave a bunch of sinful people (beginning with Moses and the Israelites at Mount Sinai, and continuing on through today) a set of rules that reveal to us our place and purpose in this world, protect us from harm, and show us our need for a Savior. We'll look at what these rules mean and how they apply to us today. I believe we'll find that the Ten Commandments are not just a list of boring dos and don'ts, but rather a road map to a victorious life of freedom and love. I invite you to join me in this journey.

YOUR RELATIONSHIP WITH GOD

PART ONE

The first four of the Ten Commandments
have to do with God and how we
are to act toward Him.

NO OTHER GODS

You must not have any other gods except me.
(Exodus 20:3)

It is no wonder that God gave this commandment to us first, because this is the rule on which all the rest are built. It is the cornerstone of rules, to be sure. Without it, there would be no way for us even to try to follow rules two through ten. As you read in the Introduction, just before He gave the Ten Commandments to Moses, God explained several things to us: He is without beginning or end, He is our Creator, He is Ruler of all that exists, and He is the One who personally delivers us from the enemy and sets us free to live full and rewarding lives. Since God has always been all these things to us, He now tells us of our first obligation: We are to keep Him number one in our lives. "Number one" means that He is the one and only, the very center of who we are and the envelope that surrounds all we do. That doesn't mean He is to be kept first in a long list of other gods. No, He is the one and *only* God, the very foundation of who we are and what we give ourselves to. And we as His people are to live in light of this reality.

TAKE IT PERSONALLY

As you begin to ponder this rule, notice the very choice words God uses to address us: *you*. He didn't say, "All My people must not have any other gods except Me." Instead, He said, "*You* must not have any other gods except Me" (emphasis added). God uses a personal, singular noun, speaking to us individually and directly—not as a big group of His followers but as unique individuals. God bases His rules on the fact that His relationship with us is real and personal. He really loves us and cares for us as individual people, for all our particular

3

desires and needs, down to the very smallest of things. And from that personal relationship, God asks us to make a radical choice: Will you love Him alone?

THE THREE A'S

This command has to do with what I'll call the three A's—admiration, affection, and allegiance. With this rule God asks each of us, "Whom do you admire?" "Who has your affection?" "Who has your allegiance?" To each of these questions, our answer must wholeheartedly be: God and God alone. Like me, you might be thinking, *But there are so many people I admire, love, and am loyal to! Is that wrong?* Not necessarily. I'll be honest; this is probably the single hardest commandment to follow. Why is that? Because there are so many things that sneak up and overtake our primary and singular love for God.

For me, there are a bunch of things that compete for my admiration, affection, and allegiance to God. Some days it might be my wife, my job, money, a new car, a new computer, more camera equipment, my friends, or even my church. What

WHAT COMPETES FOR YOUR ADMIRATION, AFFECTION, AND ALLEGIANCE?

_____

_____

_____

_____

_____

competes for your admiration, affection, and allegiance? Your girlfriend or boyfriend? Making the honor roll? Being popular at school? Music? Simply having fun? New clothes or worrying about the way you look? Are any of these things bad in and of themselves? Not at all, but they can consume our attention to the exclusion of making God the axis of our lives, becoming sin as they push God down on our list of priorities. But all these things are definitely a part of our lives, right? So how is it possible to live our lives fully and also make God the sole priority of our admiration, affection, and allegiance? Allow me to give you an example or two from my own life.

PRIORITIES

When I was in high school, I was pretty consumed with having fun. You see, I wasn't the best student, and doing well in my classes took a lot of work. I had friends, however, who always did their homework quickly and for whom making the honor roll seemed the easiest thing in the world. Not me. For me to pull a C on a test would require hours and hours of hard work studying, paying super-close attention in class, and tons of note taking. I always envied my friends who made school seem so easy and who always had plenty of time for fun.

Since I wanted to enjoy myself too, there came a point when I quit trying to work and decided to make having fun at school my goal. And fun I had. I soon became known as the class clown. Always quick with a joke, making fun of the teachers behind their backs, sleeping in class, or daydreaming, I was consumed with having the most fun I could during high school. Being such a "fun guy," other people in my classes would often invite me to parties to hang out and have "fun." I loved that I was the life of the party, as it were. But my pursuit led me to underage drinking and other behavior that compromised my beliefs and certainly interfered with God being my number one priority in life.

WHAT ARE YOUR TOP FIVE PRIORTIES?

_____

_____

_____

_____

_____

In high school I was also fascinated with being in love. I loved to be in love. I would often sit in class and dream of a girl who had captured my interest, or if I happened to be in a relationship at the time, I would spend most of my time in class writing my girlfriend notes (when I wasn't joking around), telling her how beautiful she was and how she meant the world to me. I would go out of my way to see her during breaks, making myself late to the next class, and would spend hours dreaming up the perfect date to impress her and further win her heart. I allowed myself to become consumed with my romantic endeavors. As the majority of the girls I dated during the earlier part of high school were not Christians, these relationships also compromised my beliefs and further distracted me from my relationship with God.

It wasn't that I consciously decided not to love God and not to make Him my sole priority in life. It's just that so much of my time and energy was spent trying to have fun and be in love with girls, I allowed things to sneak up on me and distract me from what my first love and obligation should have been. As I look back, I truly do believe that if my constant priority had been to have God in the number one spot in my heart, I would have made different choices and the outcome would have been quite different. Are there things or people in your life that have crept up on you and become a god to you?

The bottom line to this (and every) rule is love. So what does it mean to love God? In this day and age, the word *love* is mainly used to express emotion that is tied to affection. A new pet brings a sense of affection, and it would be appropriate to say that you *love* your pet. You might even say that you love your new video game. And of course, if you meet someone, s/he is very good-looking, and you are drawn to be with them, you might even say that you have *fallen in love.* Love can be emotional, with earthly connection and inspiration, like loving your parents because they care for you. If you are in church and the worship band is totally rocking or your pastor gives a very stirring message, you might very well say without hesitation that you *love* God. Is this what it means to love God? Well, partially. Loving God *can* be an emotional experience. But there is so much more to it than that.

WHAT DO YOU LOVE?

A RADICAL CHOICE (NOT JUST EMOTION)

What does it mean to love God? Well, let's look at a few things the Bible has to say about that. We'll start with Deuteronomy 6:5: "Love the LORD your God with all your heart, all your soul, and all your strength." In John 14:15 Jesus says, "If you love me, you will obey my commands." And finally, we find in 1 John 4:20a, and 21b, "If people say, 'I love God,' but hate their brothers or sisters, they are liars. . . . Those who love God must also love their brothers and sisters." From these three passages, it appears that love of God involves our whole being, thoughts, and actions. It means not allowing possessions or pursuits to take over our lives and distract us from God. It means obeying His commands, which requires first knowing what they are—something gained through reading the Bible. It also means loving those around us, which can certainly be difficult at times.

This kind of love involves radical choices. God tells us to love Him and trust Him no matter what, and He has certainly given us more than enough reason to love Him and to choose not to have other gods except Him. But I am easily distracted, thinking about how I wish I had a bigger house, how I sounded really smart when talking to a friend the other day, how I would rather watch television than visit my elderly neighbor whose house smells funny. Within about ten seconds, love of things and of self can take over my mind and heart.

> **WHAT DISTRACTS YOU FROM LOVING GOD?**
>
> _____
> _____
> _____
> _____
> _____
> _____
> _____

Remember, though, that we are not alone in this. After Jesus says that loving Him means obeying His commands, He adds that the Father will give us a Helper (the Holy Spirit) to be with us. We can ask the Spirit to work in us and change our hearts so we do not put other gods before Him. Also, the more we know of God, the more we will be drawn to love Him, and the more our earthly distractions will pale in comparison to His will and love for us. So be sure to spend time with Him, learn about Him, acknowledge who He is, ask Him for help, and thank Him. In keeping with His Word, you will find yourself loving Him because He first loved you.

DEPENDENCE AND RELIANCE

Love and dependence often go hand in hand. We love those we depend on, and we depend on those we love. Think of your relationships with your parents or your friends. Your love for and dependence on them are probably intertwined. What other things do we depend on? Our looks? What people think of us? Our possessions? There are so many things in modern society to which we've enslaved ourselves—technology, medicine, money, appearances. It is easy to let these things rule us and to become, in a sense, our gods. That is why this commandment applies to us today as much as it has to people at any other time in history.

Unfortunately, the things or people we choose to rely on will often let us down. God tells us and proves to us throughout the Bible and throughout our lives that we can trust and depend on Him. As we rely on God, we will continue to see His character and His love for us. We've talked about how God wants us to be free; this is part of why He gives us this commandment. Only through loving, relying, and depending on God do we find true liberation and freedom.

WHAT DO YOU DEPEND ON?

CONCLUSION

Let's remember, God is the one thing we are to base our lives on. Look to God solely; love God wholly. Live with God, and lean on God. Everything else will fall into the right place in your life. Do this, and you will be on your way to pursuing the first rule for freedom in life.

the **RULES**

**FIVE THINGS I WILL CHANGE ABOUT
THE WAY I LIVE WITH GOD ARE:**

1.
2.
3.
4.
5.

AMERICAN IDOLS

You must not make for yourselves an idol that looks like anything in the sky above or on the earth below or in the water below the land. You must not worship or serve any idol, because I, the LORD your God, am a jealous God. If you hate me, I will punish your children, and even your grandchildren and great-grandchildren. But I show kindness to thousands who love me and obey my commands.

(EXODUS 20:4–6)

We know from our first rule that we must worship God and God alone. That rule seems obvious for those of us who are Christians, and it makes perfect sense. So what's the deal with the second rule? "You must not make for yourselves an idol that looks like anything in the sky above or on the earth below or in the water below the land. You must not worship or serve any idol." It sure seems like a no-brainer, especially in this day and age. We're probably not acquainted with a single person who bows down before an inanimate object, such as a statue, and worships it. There are members of religions who do, literally, bow down in front of statues to express their devotion to false gods. But are they actually worshiping the statue itself? In some cases yes, but in most cases no. They are expressing their devotion to what that statue represents. Let's look at the context in which God originally gave this rule and see how it compares to our world today.

> **i*dol,** n.—(1) an image or other material object representing a deity and worshiped as such; (2) a deity other than God; (3) a person or thing devotedly or excessively admired; (4) a mere image or semblance of something visible but without substance; (5) a false notion; fallacy. *(Random House Webster's College Dictionary)*

HOW QUICKLY WE FORGET

In the time the Old Testament was written, the society that surrounded God's people, the Israelites, were full of people serving many different gods, represented by objects made of wood, stone, or metal. The Israelites regularly succumbed to the temptation to conform to those around them. Hmm . . . this sounds familiar. Though peer pressure is most commonly associated with young people, we all feel some pressure to be like those around us or others we think are cool. We often incorporate the ideas and philosophies of our peers into our own lives.

WHO ARE THE COOLEST STUDENTS AT YOUR SCHOOL?

_____

_____

_____

_____

_____

The people of Israel were quick to forget God's promises and what He had done for them in the past. Throughout their journey away from Egypt, the Israelites often gave up on God even though He had performed many great miracles to free them from slavery. But God promised Moses on Mount Sinai, "I will live with the people of Israel and be their God. And they will know that I am the LORD their God who led them out of Egypt so that I could live with them. I am the LORD their God" (Exodus 29:45–46). Exodus 32:1 tells us, "The people saw that a long time had passed and Moses had not come down from the mountain. So they gathered around Aaron and said, 'Moses led us out of Egypt, but we don't know what has happened to him. Make us gods who will lead us.'" So they melted down their gold jewelry and made a golden calf, to which they offered sacrifices and worship. Just like the Israelites, people in our day are looking for something or someone to follow. And also just like the Israelites, we can become very impatient and turn to people or ideologies other than God when things aren't going the way we think they should.

Now, it wasn't just the worship of other gods that God hated. He also did not want His people to make earthly representations of Himself, the one true God. It makes complete sense why it would tick God off to see His people all hunkered down and drooling over a phony god made of wood or gold. But what if we created something that represented the one true God, what does God think about that?

PICTURES OR PRIORITIES?

Timmy is almost four years old, and he loves his mom. Timmy loves his mom so much that one afternoon he pulled up a chair to the kitchen table, and with his box of jumbo crayons clutched tightly in his chubby hands, he sat down to make her a picture. With great determination, Timmy first grabbed a big brown crayon. With much effort, he managed to scrawl the outline of his dear mother's face, roughly in the shape of a lumpy potato. He grabbed a green crayon next for the eyes. He'd heard his dad say on several occasions that his mother had eyes the color of emeralds. Timmy didn't know what an emerald was, but he knew what the color green looked like, and her eyes seemed to be about the same. Two big circles were drawn within the lumpy potato head to represent his mom's eyes. Next came her nose, so that time a yellow crayon appeared, but how do you draw one? Timmy drew a circle underneath and between the two eyes. In the nose-circle, he drew two small vertical lines to represent her nostrils. Aha! Her nose! Now for the lips. Red, of course. Timmy searched his box for the right shade of red and pulled one out. "Fire Engine Red," it said. *Close enough,* thought Timmy. One more circle beneath the nose appeared and the mouth was made. All that was left was the hair. Black for

Timmy's mom's hair, which was long and straight. Timmy drew long black sprouts from the top of the lumpy potato head, and the hair was finished.

With a long sigh of satisfaction, Timmy leaned back in his chair and stared at his drawing with great delight. "A picture of my mommy," he said out loud to himself.

All of a sudden, the back door swung open and in walked Timmy's mother from her work in the garden. With a start, Timmy grabbed his drawing, ran to her side, and shoved the picture in her face. "See what I just made for you, Mommy? It's a picture of you!" What was Timmy's mom's reaction? I would guess that she scooped her young son up in her arms, held and kissed him and told him how wonderful his drawing was, and then taped it prominently to the refrigerator for anyone to see. The drawing didn't look anything like her, not even vaguely human, but she would have recognized his gesture as a feeble attempt to express his love and admiration for her, and she would respond with love herself. Are we not the same as Timmy? Would we not be like a small child, scribbling in wonder of a big and powerful God? Wouldn't God be pleased with such a simple effort and sincere intentions? I believe He would. But some people would say, and even argue, that this is wrong and most displeasing to God. That with this rule we should never, ever make any kind of image that represents God. But sadly, that argument misses the whole point. What *does* this rule mean for us?

Let's remember our definition of an idol. An idol is something that takes the place of the one true God. It has to do with what or who has our admiration, affection, and allegiance. Did little Timmy allow his picture to take the place the place of his mother? Did he begin to love a piece of paper and his own scribbling more than his own mother? Certainly not. Can you think of an instance where you took the time to make a small statue or painting which took the place of God in your life? Probably not. So then how does this rule apply to you and me? It tells us that we are not to work to make anything of this world more important than God. Or another way, we are not to worship anything that is of this world.

Consider this. Worship has to do with making a sacrifice. Worship is work. Let's ask ourselves this question: What are the things we sacrifice and work for? Take schoolwork, for instance. Let's say that you are a person who gets extremely good grades in school. Have you ever found yourself making big sacrifices in order to devote yourself to your studies and maintaining your GPA? Has that GPA become a 'god' in your life? It doesn't have to be. There is a big difference in doing your best work at school out of your love and devotion to God rather than for your own pride and ego. If you are a gifted student, know that you are able exercise the gifts He has given you and do all your work to His honor and glory.

There are so many little things in each of our lives that tend to climb up our priorities list and consume our attention more than God, and this is not acceptable to Him. God does not want us to devote ourselves to anything less than Him. This rule also requires that we actually *know* God and worship Him truly.

MISTAKEN IDENTITY

God wants to be known for who He really is. We all want others to know us, like us, and want to hang out with us because of who we really are and not for being something we aren't.

One day a few years back, I was running around town doing some errands for my job, and I finished sooner than I had expected. As I headed back to my office, I passed a music studio that I visited often for work. Since I was a frequent customer of theirs, knew all the people who worked there, and had become good friends with many of them, I decided to drop in unannounced for a quick visit. It had been a few months since I'd been there, and in my absence I had grown a goatee. I was also wearing a ball cap that day.

As I entered the front door, I spotted Denny, the owner of the studio, in the back room and offered him a friendly wave. I then started toward the receptionist to say hello, but what happened next, I never would have expected. Denny came bursting out from the back room toward me, almost at a run. As he walked quickly in my direction, he had the biggest grin on his face, and he hollered out to me, "I am *sooo* glad to see you. I am so honored that you would drop in on us unannounced!"

HAVE YOU EVER PRETENDED TO BE SOMETHING YOU'RE NOT SO PEOPLE WOULD LIKE YOU MORE?

_____

_____

_____

_____

Wow, I thought. I knew Denny was a great guy, but I didn't expect such an enthusiastic reaction to my impromptu visit. As he neared me, his pace slowed down a bit, and I saw a different look creep across his face. "Oh, hey, Mark. How are you doing?" he said, much less enthusiastically. We exchanged pleasantries, then Denny went back to work. It seemed a bit weird, but whatever. Later, I asked someone about Denny's strange greeting. "Oh," they laughed. "Denny thought you were Garth Brooks when you first walked in."

Then it all made sense. Garth Brooks was also a frequent customer of theirs. I had a goatee on my face, just like Garth had at the time, and I was wearing a ball cap, just like he often wore. But the truth is, I was a bit offended and insulted. Not because I was mistaken for Garth Brooks, but because when Denny first came to say hello, he had made me feel like the most special person in the world. As he realized that I wasn't who he thought I was, his greeting changed from enthusiastic to cordial. I wasn't as important to him as he had initially made me feel. And that's cool. Sure, I wasn't the biggest-selling recording artist of all time like Garth Brooks. I was just some kid who worked a nine-to-five job at a small Christian record label. But I wanted him to be excited about seeing me—as the person I really was.

Just like my visit to the recording studio, God wants us to know and worship Him for who He truly is, and not for someone He is not. It is unacceptable not to know and worship the true God.

KNOWLEDGE + FAITH = TRUE WORSHIP

It is only appropriate that God, being the object of our worship, would have thoughts about how He wants us to worship Him. God wants to be known by us and known for who He is. What do we learn when we *really* get to know people? We get to know their hearts, how they think, their characteristics, interests, mannerisms, temperaments, and dispositions. How do we get to know someone? Well, we spend time with them, observe them, and listen to them. How are we to know God rightly so that we may worship Him? This seems difficult because we cannot see God with our eyes. God is a spirit (John 5:24). He does not physically exist within the realm we know as creation. God is the master of creation and exists above and beyond all that we can see. John 1:18 says, "No one has ever seen God." Well, fortunately for us, it is immediately followed by these words: "But God the only Son [Jesus] is very close to the Father, and he has shown us what God is like." We've seen God's heart, thoughts, and actions through the life of Jesus, communicated to us in the Bible. God's Word tells us the story of who He is and what He is doing, and God's Spirit enables us to understand His Word. In addition to knowing God through the Bible, we are to be in constant communication with Him through prayer.

WHO DO YOU KNOW BEST IN THE WORLD?
WHAT IS S/HE LIKE?

We each have the responsibility and privilege of learning who God is so that we may worship Him rightly. It is also the responsibility of churches to teach and remind their congregations of who God is, based on what He reveals in His Word and not on our feeble imaginations. God gives us faith to receive and believe His Word, allowing us to worship Him in truth.

A JEALOUS GOD

God tells us that He is a jealous God. Offhand, that doesn't sound like a very good thing for God to be, so what does it mean for God to be jealous? Two definitions of the word *jealous* in the *Random House Webster's College Dictionary* are: "watchful in guarding something" and "intolerant of unfaithfulness or rivalry." These two definitions both seem to fit. God fiercely guards His authority and His name. We also know that He demands complete faithfulness. We've already talked in the first rule about how God regards rivals for our affection and allegiance to Him. God is jealous of any worship that is not directed to who He truly is. Jesus tells us, "God is spirit, and those who worship him must worship in spirit and truth" (John 4:24). If we are not bowing down in worship to the one true God, we are bowing down in worship to something other than God. This is spiritual adultery—the leaving of our first love in exchange for something else.

PUNISHMENT

If you hate me, I will punish your children, and even your grandchildren and great-grandchildren. (Exodus 20:5b)

God equates false worship (idolatry) of Himself with hating Him. We'll look one more time at the severity of this sin and see why we are all accountable. Romans 1:19–23, 25 states:

God shows his anger because some knowledge of him has been made clear to them. . . . So people have no excuse for the bad things they do. They knew God, but they did not give glory to God or thank him. Their thinking became useless. Their foolish minds were filled with darkness. They said they were wise, but they became fools. They traded the glory of God who lives forever for the worship of idols made to look like earthly people, birds, animals, and snakes. . . . They traded the truth of God for a lie. They worshiped and served what had been created instead of the God who created those things, who should be praised forever.

It follows that God would want to punish someone who is guilty of the idolatry described in this passage. Let's explore for a minute how it proceeds to the future generations.

HAVE YOU PICKED UP ANY BAD HABITS FROM YOUR FAMILY?

If a father or mother worships someone or something other than God, they will likely pass it along to their children. It is not necessarily that God is punishing the children for the sins of their parents, but we can guess that children will imitate this improper and sinful form of worship in their families. And their children will most likely do the same, and so on. If this family heritage of false worship continues, it should be of no surprise that God will punish all those involved, even if they don't know any better. God's punishment is designed to turn hearts back to the truth. Once a pattern like this is established, it takes a mighty move of God, a miracle, to break the wrong cycle and turn hearts back to the truth. This gives us a good idea of why God said that He will punish succeeding generations.

PASS IT DOWN

But I show kindness to thousands who love me and obey my commands. (Exodus 20:6)

In contrast to the punishment for families who continue in their worship of anything other than God, those who do love, obey, and worship God in spirit and in truth receive God's rich blessing. God's devotion to His people runs deep, and He loves to show kindness to them. Think of a family that is dedicated to worshiping God properly. As that family continues to grow and passes down true worship to subsequent generations, there are a vast number of people who honor God with their worship and their lives. Thousands upon thousands of people will truly know God and be blessed by Him. Remember back to the idea of peer pressure as it applies to the worship of God? Think about this: If there is a handful of people who love God and strive to obey God's rules by worshiping Him in the right way, wouldn't that obedience, love, and true worship naturally spread to others? If outsiders were to witness God's life-changing power of true worship in your life, do you not think they would follow? Of course they would. Think. It starts with just one person, and that person should be you.

GOD'S LOVE

In addition to asserting God's authority, all the rules in this book have the common theme of reflecting God's love for us.

Let's look for a minute at how rule two reveals God's interest in what is best for us. In a few chapters, we'll examine how physical adultery is a distortion of God's loving plan for us that can lead to great pain. The worship of anything or anyone other than the true God is basically spiritual adultery and will ultimately lead to great disappointment. Idols are powerless and will let us down. Psalm 115:3–7 illustrates this point:

> Our God is in heaven.
>> He does what he pleases.
> Their idols are made of silver and gold,
>> the work of human hands.
> They have mouths, but they cannot speak.
>> They have eyes, but they cannot see.
> They have ears, but they cannot hear.
>> They have noses, but they cannot smell.
> They have hands, but they cannot feel.
>> They have feet, but they cannot walk.
> No sounds come from their throats.

Isaiah 44:9*a* says, "Some people make idols, but they are worth nothing. People treasure them, but they are useless." God wants us to rely on the One who is powerful, who can help us, and who is able to save us.

CONCLUSION

We also know that the Son of God has come and has given us understanding so that we can know the True One. And our lives are in the True One and in his Son, Jesus Christ. He is the true God and the eternal life. So, dear children, keep yourselves away from gods [idols]. (1 John 5:20–21)

This rule teaches us to be wary in what we worship and the way we worship. Don't substitute the truth of God for a lie or anything less than God Himself. God has given us some very real ways to know Him so that we can worship Him for who He really is. We should seek to know God through the Bible and the story of Jesus' life and communicate with Him through prayer. Do this, and see God's blessing become evident in your life; break this rule, and you will know firsthand the punishment that comes from a jealous God.

FIVE WAYS I'LL CHANGE MY LIFE TO ELIMINATE IDOLS ARE:

1. _____

2. _____

3. _____

4. _____

5. _____

WATCH YOUR MOUTH

You must not use the name of the LORD your God thoughtlessly; the LORD will punish anyone who misuses his name.

(EXODUS 20:7)

When you pick up a phone and dial a number, what happens when the person on the other end of the line answers your call? In most cases, you say hello and identify yourself. And how do you identify yourself? Do you tell the person every single detail that describes you—where you live, what you look like, how old you are, what your likes and dislikes are, if you are a good or bad student, who your friends are, etc.? No. There's a much more efficient way to identify yourself: You say your name. It's quick, it's simple, and depending on how well that person on the other end knows you, it can conjure up all the details that describe you. Our names are a gathering point of knowledge and information, and they tend to sum up who we are. If I bring up the name Bill Clinton, what springs to your mind? Probably a former president of the United States who served two consecutive terms, has gray hair, speaks with a mild southern drawl, has a wife named Hillary and a daughter named Chelsea, got into big trouble when he lied about an extramarital relationship with a White House intern, and was impeached by Congress. Names have the power to evoke vivid images of what we know or imagine a person to be. It will even determine how we use that name. In this chapter, and with this rule, we are going to investigate God, His names, and how we should or should not speak His names.

WHAT DOES YOUR NAME MEAN?

NAMESAKE

When your parents named you as a baby, they had some reason to name you what they did. In this day and age, it is common for parents to choose a certain name because they think it sounds cool. They are looking to achieve a certain aesthetic or individuality. I have a number of friends who have chosen names like Skye, Buster, or Soleil for their babies for the sake of being unique and different.

Other parents prefer names that have meaning to them personally, choosing to name a child after a relative, a close friend, or someone well-known whom they admire. A common practice among Christians is to name a child after a person from biblical times who was a positive role model in the service of God. In a country like the United States that was founded on Judeo-Christian principles, look at the massive popularity of the names John, David, Peter, Paul, Sarah, Mary, and Ruth throughout the years. Through these names, parents intend to associate a particular spiritual quality with their child.

But going back to biblical times, names carried much greater importance, significance, and meaning than they do today. Back then, names were given to people to provide specific meaning and direction for their entire lives. They were meant to explain people's personalities and characters. Consider for instance, Abraham, whose original name was Abram. Abram and his wife were old and not able to have children, but God desired to bless Abram and make him the father of many people. God wanted to give a special meaning to Abram and the rest of his life, so He made him a promise and changed his name. In Genesis 17:5–6, God said, "I am changing your name from Abram to Abraham because I am making you a father of many nations. I will give you many descendants. New nations will be born from you, and kings will come from you." Abram's original name means "exalted father," but the new name God gave, Abraham, means "father of a multitude." God also changed the name of Abraham's wife from Sarai to Sarah. Both mean "princess," but her new name implied that there would be noble descendants in her future (see Genesis 17:15-16).

There are examples of names with significant meanings in the New Testament as well. In Luke 1:13, an angel of the Lord told Zacharias that he and his barren wife, Elizabeth, would have a son and instructed that he be named John, which means "The Lord is gracious." During His time on earth, Jesus Himself assigned a new name to His disciple Simon. When Simon recognized that Jesus is Christ, the Son of the living God, Jesus gave him the name Peter, which means "rock," saying, "On this rock I will build my church" (Matthew 16:18). Since the Scripture makes it quite clear that names are important to God, let's look at God's name and find out what it means.

BASED ON MEANING, WHAT WOULD YOU WANT GOD TO CHANGE YOUR NAME TO?

THE NAMES OF GOD

In Psalm 8, King David starts off by saying, "LORD our Lord, your name is the most wonderful name in all the earth! It brings you praise in heaven above." What did David know that caused him to say that God's name was the very best name in all the earth? How could God's name be so good that it brings praise not only on earth but also in heaven? It is because of what the name of God means—both by definition and by reputation. Let's look at two of the primary names for God in the Old Testament and their meanings, then the one name for God given in the New Testament.

Yahweh

In the third chapter of Exodus, God speaks to Moses, instructing him on how to deliver the Israelites out of captivity in Egypt. It is here that God tells Moses what His name is and what it means.

> But Moses said to God, "I am not a great man! How can I go to the king [of Egypt] and lead the Israelites out of Egypt?"
>
> God said, "I will be with you. This will be the proof that I am sending you: After you lead the people out of Egypt, all of you will worship me on this mountain."
>
> Moses said to God, "When I go to the Israelites, I will say to them, 'The God of your fathers sent me to you.' What if the people say, 'What is his name?' What should I tell them?"
>
> Then God said to Moses, "I AM WHO I AM. When you go to the people of Israel, tell them, 'I AM sent me to you. . . .' This will always be my name, by which people from now on will know me." (Exodus 3:11–14, 15b)

God refers to himself as "I AM WHO I AM" or, more simply, "I AM," which we translate into English as *Yahweh* or, more commonly, *Jehovah*. (In your Bible you will probably find His name shown as "LORD," as in the Psalm 8 passage mentioned earlier.) Talk about a complicated name. I AM WHO I AM? What does that mean? It is as if God is talking in circles and then telling us that is His name. But I believe that is precisely His point. God is telling us that there is *nothing* to compare Himself to, except Himself. And since names are meant to identify, how else would God identify Himself but by using

Himself as a reference? *Yahweh* is the proper name of the God of Israel and is used 6,824 times in the Old Testament.

> ## WHY IS IT IMPORTANT THAT GOD CANNOT BE COMPARED TO ANYTHING OTHER THAN HIMSELF?
>
> _____
>
> _____
>
> _____
>
> _____

Since the name *Yahweh*, or "I AM WHO I AM," is virtually impossible to comprehend by itself, we must look to God's character through word and deed in order to understand it. In the passage above, God first tells Moses, "I will be with you." God is a God of promises. He assures Moses that as he obeys God and leads the children of Israel out of captivity, God will be right there with them. He is a faithful friend and He will not abandon His children, even today. This gives us some understanding of what the name *Yahweh* means. God is faithful and trustworthy and promises never to leave us.

We could go on looking at other implied meanings of the name *Yahweh*, but there are other names for God used in the Bible that have more specific meaning. These other names also refer to the one true God and will help us understand even more about our God and His character.

Elohim

Elohim is a name used for God more than 2,500 times in the Old Testament. It refers to His divine attributes, such as unlimited power, governing authority, and His work of creation, among others. When you read your Bible and see the word *God*, it almost always is the translation for *Elohim*. So God's introduction to our first rule in Exodus 20:2 would read like this: "I am the LORD [*Yahweh*—who He is] your God [*Elohim*—what He does], who brought you out of the land of Egypt where you were slaves." There are a few meanings for Elohim in this verse. God is a deliverer, and since He is about to start giving us our list of rules, He is also the lawgiver.

As you read the Bible, you will find many great examples of the meaning of God/*Elohim*. In Jonah 1:9, God is referred to as the Creator, and in Psalm 50:6, God is described as the Judge. In Jeremiah 10:10, we see that God is King and Ruler. Our God is so big and His deeds are so vast that the best way to get to know Him better is to read the many stories of His actions throughout the Bible. When you read those stories, take time to ponder all the different attributes of God in order to gain some understanding of how majestic our God truly is.

WHY IS JESUS' NAME SIGNIFICANT?

_____

_____

_____

Jesus Christ

Now let's take a look at our God who became human and walked on this earth with us, Jesus Christ, and see how His name came about and what it means. In Matthew 1:21, the angel of the Lord told Joseph about Mary: "She will give birth to a son, and you will name him Jesus, because he will save his people from their sins." In Luke 1:31-33, an angel of the Lord told Mary that she would give birth to a son, ". . . and you will name him Jesus. He will be great and will be called the Son of the Most High. The Lord God will give him the throne of King David, his ancestor. He will rule over the people of Jacob forever, and his kingdom will never end."

The name *Jesus* means "Yahweh is salvation." The word *Christ* refers to the fact that Jesus is the "Messiah" or "Anointed One," whose arrival had been expected for centuries. The Jews of Jesus' time were anticipating a Messiah who would be an earthly king and would free them from the Roman Empire. Instead, the Christ who came in the person of Jesus was a heavenly King who freed the world from the consequences of sin and gave them eternal life.

When we refer to God, the Lord, or Jesus Christ, we are speaking of the one true God. With any mention of His names come the full power and authority and kindness and compassion and provision and glory and majesty and honor of the God of the Bible, who is still very present and active today. That is what gives such overwhelming weight to our speech when we so much as say the word *God*.

SAY THE NAME

We have taken a good look at the significance of names, especially those of God, so now let's get back to our rule: "You must not use the name of the LORD [*Yahweh*] your God [*Elohim*] thoughtlessly; the LORD will punish anyone who misuses his name" (Exodus 20:7).

This third rule to live by also involves the worship of God. It informs us of the seriousness, gravity, and majesty that are due God—even with the mention of His name. That's pretty big stuff. Who else demands so much respect that they will dictate the context of the mention of their name? Only God. Through this commandment, God again asserts that He is God. He is the only thing worthy of our wholehearted devotion and worship, even as we speak His name.

So what are the ways in which people use the name of God thoughtlessly or wrongly? The first way is probably the most obvious and the most offensive to God and Christians alike.

Blasphemy

Blasphemy is to speak evil of God, to slander God, or to deny giving God credit for good, which we should attribute to Him. This is the ultimate form of verbal disrespect to God. To blaspheme God, one must first know of some aspects of God's character or reputation and then turn around and deny those very same aspects. You don't just do it accidentally. It is like dragging God's name through the mud. The book of Leviticus (24:10-23) tells of a man who got into a fight with an Israelite, and during the fight he started cursing the Lord. The rest of the people watching were so shocked that they took him prisoner and brought him before Moses to be punished. So great and offensive was his sin that God told Moses to have him stoned to death. There are many more instances of blasphemy throughout the Bible, some from God's enemies, but also from His very own children, who turned and denied the goodness and providence of God. Do we who are living in the twenty-first century often curse God directly or knowingly and willfully deny His very attributes and actions? Yes. Do we curse God indirectly or unintentionally and carelessly deny His attributes and actions? Even more so.

> **DO YOU CUSS SOME, A LOT, TOO MUCH?**
>
> _____
>
> _____
>
> _____

Profanity

Modern profanity is not usually intended to be blasphemous. People use the names of God and Jesus Christ as interjections or exclamations in circumstances of shock, surprise, and anger. People use these names to add force to their words. Why? Because these names hold so much more weight than any other name that they cannot be denied. No one I have ever met would, if they slammed their hand in a car door, scream out, "J. Lo!"—though I might find the randomness of that quite amusing! I do know some (usually those who don't consider themselves Christians, but sometimes even those who do) who might scream out the name of Jesus, however, and that is never funny.

I hear it so often, you would think I would be used to it by now. In the movies, on television, or even from people we know, we hear the most dreadful words fly out of their mouths and into our ears. No, it's not the big "F" word or any of the other highly colorful, four-letter variety; the inappropriate use of God's name is much more offensive to the God we serve. When someone utters the name of God, closely followed by a curse, or says the very name of Jesus Christ in a context that is harsh and lacks love or understanding of who Jesus is, I know that I am deeply offended, and I would trust that other Christians, as well as God Himself, are deeply saddened by it as well.

Even without blasphemy or profanity, many Christians are guilty of breaking this rule all the time, but in subtler and less obvious ways.

Speaking for God

Do you use the name of God to support ideas, agendas, and plans that may or may not come directly from God? Have you ever heard someone start off a sentence with: "The Lord told me that we are supposed to . . ." or end a sentence with ". . . and this is the will of God"? I've even heard of people who choose to break up with their girlfriend or boyfriend because "God told them to." In some cases this might be true, but often it is just a convenient excuse that might sound good and spiritual. If it is not true, it is the most dangerous way to back out of a relationship. Never, ever use God as an easy way to get what you want. This is certainly an example of taking God's name in vain! Christians are often quick to become God's mouthpiece and speak of what they think is God's will. When someone claims they know God's specific will for a certain situation, how can that be argued? We do know that God has spoken to man throughout the ages and given man direction, but whenever we speak *for* God in any situation, we had better be right. A lot of hurt and confusion can be caused by this type of invocation of God's name and will when not done with the utmost care, discernment, and prayer.

WHEN HAVE YOU EVER SPOKEN FOR GOD?

_____

_____

_____

_____

_____

Trivializing

The biggest way that evangelical Christians in America thoughtlessly misuse the name of the Lord is by trivial use. It happens so much around us that we don't even notice it anymore. One example of this was pretty popular just a few years ago. Anywhere you were driving, you could spot car bumpers with a simple little sticker that claimed, "Jesus is my copilot." Taken at face value, it is true that Jesus is indeed with us and helps us Christians everywhere we go. But if we stop and think about this a bit more, we are taking the name of Jesus and *all* He represents to us (our Creator, our Redeemer, our Advocate to God the Father, our role model, etc.) and simplifying it all down to a slogan that says, in effect, "Jesus is a guy who helps me out." Even worse, those bumper stickers had a more glaring fault than what we have just talked about. Jesus is *my* copilot. Whoops! Shouldn't that be the other way around? For anyone to call themselves a Christian (which means "a follower of Christ") and have a bumper sticker on their car that implies that *they* are in control and not Jesus, now that is certainly embarrassing.

A great many companies exist to sell merchandise like T-shirts, music, videos, posters, bumper stickers, breath mints, bracelets, and yes, even books like the one you are reading, to Christians. This is not a bad thing, because sometimes the products are beneficial to deepening our relationship with God. But sometimes these companies will cross the line and use the name of God, Jesus, or His awesome works as a catchy slogan to make us run out and purchase something. This is something to be aware of because this rule teaches us to be responsible to God by honoring and respecting His name and His reputation.

HAVE YOU EVER SEEN AN EXAMPLE OF SOMEONE TRIVIALIZING CHRIST?

_____

_____

_____

_____

It is easy to point the finger at others, but what about us? Are we ever guilty of misusing God's name? Do we ourselves ever use God's name casually? How many of us flippantly say, "I swear to God . . ."? Do we ever do the name of Christ a disservice?

How many times, in the company of people who know us as a Christian, do we say or do things Jesus would be ashamed of? Is that honoring the name of Christ? Hardly.

USING IT RIGHT

We now know the importance of God's name and have looked at several scenarios of how not to use the name of God. Let's look at how we *should* speak.

Let's say that you have recently begun to date the boy or girl of your dreams, and you are in love. When you are talking with your friends about this person who is the object of your affection, what kind of words do you use? If you truly love him or her, you would tell of all the things that please you, right? Or would you insult your loved one and make a joke at his or her expense? (No way.) If you love that person you would speak earnestly and sincerely, right? Or would it be a casual, offhanded conversation in which it would appear that the person means very little to you? (Of course not.) Would you praise this person or insult this person? You see, the things that come out of our mouths expose what we think in our hearts.

WHAT DO YOU SAY THAT EXPOSES YOUR HEART?

Jesus says to His followers in Luke 6:45, "Good people bring good things out of the good they stored in their hearts. But evil people bring evil things out of the evil they stored in their hearts. People speak the things that are in their hearts."

CONCLUSION

How do *you* talk about the One who created you, knows you, and gives you your every breath and beat of your heart? How do you talk about the God who came here to earth, wrapped Himself in a human body to experience everything you and I go through, lived a blameless life, then sacrificed Himself to a gruesome death for you because of your sin? How do you speak about a God who is so powerful that death itself was shattered as He came back to life, then ascended to heaven where He controls the entirety of all creation, and who sent His very own Spirit to live in our hearts to comfort us and to help carry us through our lives? If God has truly captured our admiration, affection, and allegiance, we will speak of Him with love, respect, and great care, because that is precisely what will be in our hearts. God gave us our mouths to speak His praise

FIVE WAYS I WILL CHANGE THE WAY I SPEAK ARE :

1. _____

2. _____

3. _____

4. _____

5. _____

and to tell of His mighty deeds. We are responsible for His reputation, and we should never take our responsibility lightly.

May we follow the example of Jesus, who, in teaching us how to pray, began, "Our Father in heaven, may your name always be kept holy" (Matthew 6:9*b*).

A DAY OF REST

Remember to keep the Sabbath holy. Work and get everything done during six days each week, but the seventh day is a day of rest to honor the LORD your God. On that day no one may do any work: not you, your son or daughter, your male or female slaves, your animals, or the foreigners living in your cities. The reason is that in six days the LORD made everything—the sky, the earth, the sea, and everything in them. On the seventh day he rested. So the LORD blessed the Sabbath day and made it holy.
(EXODUS 20:8–11)

What a weird thing to find in our list of rules. God gave us a day off. He tells us not to do any work, to chill out and get some rest. Now I don't know about you, but that seems like the best rule of all to me! But if we think about it simply in terms of chilling out, somehow this rule starts to seem suspicious. Some people, myself included, have a hard time believing this is the case. Can it really be true that to follow this rule, all we have to do is kick back and relax? The answer is yes, but God does have some specific thoughts about how we are to go about getting that rest, what the purpose of rest is, and what the word *rest* really means.

THE LORD'S DAY

Sunday is the day on which most Christians celebrate the Sabbath, which we often call "the Lord's Day." And what do we do on Sundays? We go to church and Sunday school, and that takes up our whole morning. After church, we eat lunch, and after that we have the whole afternoon to catch up on schoolwork or maybe do chores around the house. If all those things are done, we might hang out with our family or friends and do something fun. Others of us may have jobs that require us to work on Sundays. Depending on the church, some of us even go back to church on Sunday night, where we'll have a youth activity before we finally finish up our day and go home to bed. All in all, Sundays are usually a day off, but we are also pretty busy on the Lord's Day. So how do we rate according to the rule? Are we successful in following it, or do we mess it up by being so busy?

WHAT ARE YOUR SUNDAYS LIKE?

_____

_____

_____

_____

_____

Keep It Holy

The rule states that we must "remember to keep the Sabbath holy." This sounds good, but do we really know what these words mean? If we were to look up the words *Sabbath* and *holy* in a Bible dictionary and insert the definitions in place of those words, the first line of our rule would read something like this: Remember to "set aside and dedicate" (holy) the "day of intermission to both celebrate and rest" (Sabbath). That helps clear the picture quite a bit. The Sabbath is an intermission, a break in the action of our regular lives. Think about going to a football game, a concert, or even a play or musical. At some point in each of these events, there is a break in the normal course of events. The purpose of the intermission is to create time to pause and take a break, reflect on what has just happened, and get charged up for what is to come. At some point during the halftime of a football game, there is a recap of the events of the first half of play and some speculation on how the second half of the game will go. This is to help us remember all the excitement and highlights of the first half and create suspense and excitement for the rest of the game. The same is true for plays, musicals, and concerts. At a play or musical, an intermission is designed to break up the story into smaller pieces so it is easier to enjoy, understand, and remember. Intermissions also give us time to stretch our legs or get a drink, allowing us a chance to be physically refreshed.

Remember

The first principle found in this rule is this: Take time to look back and remember, because that is exactly what God did before He rested. After creating Adam and Eve, in Genesis 1:31, "God looked at everything he had made, and it was very good. Evening passed, and morning came. This was the sixth day." He had just finished creating man and woman, and He wanted to take a step back and admire His handiwork. It says that when He was finished creating, He stopped and surveyed all He had done, and He called it very good.

That is the same thing He wants us to do. We are to stop what we are doing and reflect on what God has done in and through our lives. We are to remember the goodness of God in providing for our needs, both physical and spiritual. We should take time to be thankful for even the smallest of things—food, health, families, friends, and all the ways in which God makes our lives rich and meaningful. We should then certainly remember the biggest things, also, like God's faithfulness to hear and answer our prayers, His helping us walk through hard times, and especially Jesus' willingness to give away His very own life by being brutally beaten and murdered for everything you and I have ever done or ever will do wrong. This act of remembering is the starting place for our worship of God and is the perfect way to begin our rest.

Pausing to remember and reflect fits quite well with what we do on Sunday mornings at church. We gather together, singing songs of celebration and worship. We continue to learn more about what God has done and is doing through the teaching of

God's Word and though the testimony of God at work in other people's lives.

WHAT HAS GOD DONE FOR YOU LATELY?

_____

_____

_____

_____

_____

Rest

The second principle of this rule is the "rest" part. What does "rest" mean? We are called to rest, just as God did after He created the universe. Genesis 2:2-3 says, "By the seventh day God finished the work he had been doing, so he rested from all his work. God blessed the seventh day and made it a holy day, because on that day he rested from all the work he had done in creating the world." He took a day off to do nothing. But He is God, and He is all-powerful, right? So why would He need to take a day off and rest? The truth is that God didn't _need_ to rest because He truly is all-powerful and has a limitless supply of strength and energy. But since He created us, He knew that we were not all-powerful and we would need to rest. This is why God rested—to lead us by example.

God created a rhythm and pattern to all of life. Rhythm is the backbone of all creation. If you are a drummer, you will really appreciate this. Within every single part of existence,

God created a natural rhythm. Sleeping and waking, day and night, the beat of every heart, the ocean tides, the rotation of galaxies, protons and neutrons that continually circle the nucleus of every atom in an unending rhythm and pattern. Rhythm is at the literal core of all that exists. And for human beings, this rhythm of life requires rest.

HOW OFTEN DO YOU REST?

So, according to our rule, what does "rest" look like? Is it a time when we get to stay in bed all day? Probably not. Let's go back to the rule:

> On that day no one may do any work: not you, your son or daughter, your male or female slaves, your animals, or the foreigners living in your cities.

From the sound of it, we are to stop doing our work or the things that comprise the daily responsibilities of our lives. That's what we shouldn't do, but what should we be doing as part of our resting?

WHAT TO DO?

The best examples of appropriate activities for the Sabbath are found in how Jesus observed the Sabbath:

Jesus was teaching in one of the synagogues on the Sabbath day. A woman was there who, for eighteen years, had an evil spirit in her that made her crippled. Her back was always bent; she could not stand up straight. When Jesus saw her, he called her over and said, "Woman, you are free from your sickness." Jesus put his hands on her, and immediately she was able to stand up straight and began praising God.

The synagogue leader was angry because Jesus healed on the Sabbath day. He said to the people, "There are six days when one has to work. So come to be healed on one of those days, and not on the Sabbath day."

The Lord answered, "You hypocrites! Doesn't each of you untie your work animals and lead them to drink water every day—even on the Sabbath day? This woman that I healed, a daughter of Abraham, has been held by Satan for eighteen years. Surely it is not wrong for her to be freed from her sickness on a Sabbath day!" When Jesus said this, all of those who were criticizing him were ashamed, but the entire crowd rejoiced at all the wonderful things Jesus was doing. (Luke 13:10–17)

On a Sabbath day, when Jesus went to eat at the home of a leading Pharisee, the people were watching Jesus very closely. And in front of him was a man with dropsy. Jesus said to the Pharisees and experts on the law, "Is it right or wrong to heal on the Sabbath day?" But they would not answer his question. So Jesus took the man, healed him, and sent him away. Jesus said to the Pharisees and teachers of the law, "If your child or ox falls into a well on the Sabbath day, will you not pull him out quickly?" (Luke 14:1–5)

One Sabbath day, as Jesus was walking through some fields of grain, his followers began to pick some grain to eat. The

Pharisees said to Jesus, "Why are your followers doing what is not lawful on the Sabbath day?"

Jesus answered, "Have you never read what David did when he and those with him were hungry and needed food? During the time of Abiathar the high priest, David went into God's house and ate the holy bread, which is lawful only for priests to eat. And David also gave some of the bread to those who were with him."

Then Jesus said to the Pharisees, "The Sabbath day was made to help people; they were not made to be ruled by the Sabbath day. So then, the Son of Man is Lord even of the Sabbath day."

Another time when Jesus went into a synagogue, a man with a crippled hand was there. Some people watched Jesus closely to see if he would heal the man on the Sabbath day so they could accuse him.

Jesus said to the man with the crippled hand, "Stand up here in the middle of everyone."

Then Jesus asked the people, "Which is lawful on the Sabbath day: to do good or to do evil, to save a life or to kill?" But they said nothing to answer him. (Mark 2:23–3:4)

A man was lying there who had been sick for thirty-eight years. When Jesus saw the man and knew that he had been sick for such a long time, Jesus asked him, "Do you want to be well?"

The sick man answered, "Sir, there is no one to help me get into the pool when the water starts moving. While I am coming to the water, someone else always gets in before me."

Then Jesus said, "Stand up. Pick up your mat and walk." And immediately the man was well; he picked up his mat and began to walk.

The day this happened was a Sabbath day. So the Jews

said to the man who had been healed, "Today is the Sabbath. It is against our law for you to carry your mat on the Sabbath day."

But he answered, "The man who made me well told me, 'Pick up your mat and walk.'"

Then they asked him, "Who is the man who told you to pick up your mat and walk?"

But the man who had been healed did not know who it was, because there were many people in that place, and Jesus had left.

Later, Jesus found the man at the Temple and said to him, "See, you are well now. Stop sinning so that something worse does not happen to you."

Then the man left and told his people that Jesus was the one who had made him well.

Because Jesus was doing this on the Sabbath day, the Jews began to persecute him. But Jesus said to them, "My Father never stops working, and so I keep working, too."

This made the Jews try still harder to kill him. They said, "First Jesus was breaking the law about the Sabbath day. Now he says that God is his own Father, making himself equal with God!" (John 5:5–18)

From these passages of Scripture, it is apparent that Jesus truly acknowledged the Sabbath and God's laws for resting on the Sabbath. But the problem in Jesus' day, and still a problem today, was that the religious rulers had long lists of strict regulations of things that were and were not allowed on the Sabbath. And those things were in addition to what God originally intended.

Jesus observed the Sabbath in the correct way. He had no problem with healing the sick or allowing people to gather food to eat. Why? Jesus was just doing His Father's business. As we just saw above in Mark 2:27, Jesus said, "The Sabbath day was made to help people; they [people] were not made to be ruled by the Sabbath day." The business of heaven is helping people. On the Lord's Day, we are allowed to stop doing what we do vocationally and occupationally, but when presented with opportunities, we are always to continue to do God's work, which is centered on caring for others. That is the most rewarding work on earth and also the work that is never done.

WHAT DO YOU THINK IS NOT ALLOWED ON SUNDAYS?

_____

_____

_____

This rule of rest on the Lord's Day sounds easy, but as we practice it every week it seems to be quite difficult. The reason for this is that it requires one hard thing from us: surrender. God is telling us to surrender our own agendas and take up His agenda instead. God wants to bless us and provide much-needed rest, and He is honored to do so. God blessed the seventh day. He honors the day of rest. The problem is that we are a restless and unbelieving people.

Most of us think we somehow can earn God's favor and blessing through God's pleasure in our work, so we continually work ourselves into the ground in hope that God will be happy with us. This rule teaches us that is not the case. For six days we are to work to the best of our ability in the name of God, but the seventh day is a time when God wants to reward us. It is so hard for us to sit still and rest in God's goodness, because deep in our hearts we really don't believe that God's love is big and wide enough to cover us when we aren't serving Him. Know this: We can't earn God's favor. The good things God has for us are far beyond our ability to get on our own.

HOW DO YOU TRY TO EARN GOD'S FAVOR?

_____

_____

_____

Remember the story of Mary and Martha? Jesus visited these two sisters at their home. Mary sat and listened at the feet of Jesus, while Martha scurried around the house preparing a meal. Martha was quite upset that her sister was of no help, but Jesus told Martha, "Martha, Martha, you are worried and upset about many things. Only one thing is important. Mary has chosen the better thing, and it will never be taken away from her" (Luke 10:41-42). The thing that Mary chose to do was to sit, be silent, and learn from Jesus.

Think of Him. Learn from Him. Be refreshed by Him. When we are able to sit and rest in God, He has an abundance of good to give us.

CONCLUSION

Sundays are a time to look back and reflect on what the Lord has done through us and through our work during the past week. We are called to remember and also to look forward to the week ahead in anticipation of what God will do. God will restore us and refresh us, both physically and spiritually, and prepare us for our week to come.

> You must obey God's law about the Sabbath
> > and not do what pleases yourselves on that holy day.
> You should call the Sabbath a joyful day
> > and honor it as the LORD's holy day.
> You should honor it by not doing whatever you please
> > nor saying whatever you please on that day.
> Then you will find joy in the LORD. (Isaiah 58:13–14*a*)

FIVE WAYS I WILL CHANGE MY HABITS ON SUNDAY ARE:

1. _____

2. _____

3. _____

4. _____

5. _____

YOUR RELATIONSHIP WITH OTHERS

PART TWO

HONOR

LIE

STEAL NG

I NEED THIS

The last six rules to live by have to do with how
we treat our neighbors.

MOM AND POP

Honor your father and your mother so that you will live a long time in the land that the LORD your God is going to give you.

(EXODUS 20:12)

ere it is, the chapter you have been waiting for, right? Well, before you roll your eyes and let out a big, fat sigh . . .

FAMILY CONNECTION

There are very good reasons for us to examine the roles of parents and children. For one, there is no relationship that affects us through the entire span of our lives like the one we have with our parents. Second, God places great significance on families, designing the relationships we have with our parents to mirror His relationship with all humankind.

Throughout all of history, God has used families to accomplish His work here on earth and to build His kingdom in heaven. In chapter 3, we talked about how God blessed Abram, changed his name to Abraham, and selected him to be the father of many nations. Through Abraham's very own family came many well-known people of faith: Joseph, Moses, Samuel, David, Solomon, and more. This big family became an entire nation of people called the Israelites. It was directly through this line, made up of real mothers and fathers, interacting with real sons and daughters, from Abraham and Sarah all the way to Joseph and the Virgin Mary, that God came down to earth in a human body to save the world. Each generation, and each individual family, played an important role in God's story.

Impact

Parents have an enormous capacity to impact the lives of their children. Everything from the choices they make on our behalf, to who they are and what they enjoy, will likely affect our lives in both big and small ways. Let's see how this played itself out in my family. Both of my granddads liked to work with their hands. My mom's dad was a carpenter by trade, and my dad's father had a garage full of tools and loved to repair things. As it turned out, my dad became a mechanical engineer when he got out of college, and in his spare time he loved to fix things, including the cars of some older widows who went to our church. My mom was not exactly afraid to pick up a hammer herself. To this day she can drive a nail through wood even straighter than my dad can.

WHAT'S YOUR FAMILY LIKE?

My parents also loved music. When my mom was young, she taught herself to play the saxophone, the piano, and the accordion. My dad was a trumpet player who could find his way around the piano just fine. One of my favorite memories from childhood is lying in bed some nights, listening to my parents play duets on the piano after my brother, sister, and I had been tucked in. If they stopped, one of us kids would yell out a request from our bedroom to keep the concert going.

My father, ever since he was in high school, has loved the art of photography, and my mother likes to paint, mainly in watercolors. Most important, my parents to this day are very active in worshiping and serving God with their lives.

So how did we Nicholas kids turn out? Well, my brother, sister, and I have many of the same loves as our parents. Though we are very different people with different personalities, we are all avid photographers who love music and the visual arts, and we all love to build and fix things with our hands. Above all, we have committed our lives to following Christ and serving Him. As it turns out, we really are in many ways the sum of our parents' (and grandparents') rich history.

So what about you? What do your parents love and do? Do they love music? Do they encourage you to participate in sports? Do they love and serve the one true living God? Chances are, the things that matter to them may someday matter to you as well. What kinds of characteristics and values do you hope to pass on to your children?

WHAT DO YOUR PARENTS LOVE AND DO?

_____

_____

_____

_____

_____

Responsibility

With such ability to affect our lives, parents also have a huge responsibility, both to future generations and to God, to continue the story and the legacy of goodness that He began. Parents' care for their children should echo that of God for them. As God provides shelter, food, and clothing for them, they are to provide shelter, food, and clothing for us. As God protects them, they are to protect. As God loves them, they are to love. As God may correct them for wrongdoing, they may also correct us for wrongdoing. Not only must parents take care of their children's physical needs, they are to provide them with wisdom and spiritual direction that prepare them for the rest of their lives.

We see a model of spiritual guidance in King David and his son Solomon. In 1 Chronicles 22:13, David tells Solomon, "Be careful to obey the rules and laws the LORD gave Moses for Israel. If you obey them, you will have success. Be strong and brave. Don't be afraid or discouraged." And in Proverbs 4:3-9, Solomon remembers,

> When I was a young boy in my father's house
> > and like an only child to my mother,
> my father taught me and said,
> > "Hold on to my words with all your heart.
> > Keep my commands and you will live.
> Get wisdom and understanding.
> > Don't forget or ignore my words.
> Hold on to wisdom, and it will take care of you.
> > Love it, and it will keep you safe.
> Wisdom is the most important thing; so get wisdom.
> > If it costs everything you have, get understanding.
> Treasure wisdom, and it will make you great;
> > hold on to it, and it will bring you honor.
> It will be like flowers in your hair
> > and like a beautiful crown on your head."

In these passages, it is very clear that the father has encouraged his son (this also applies to mothers and daughters, of course) in the things that will truly make a difference in his life—wisdom and understanding. Parents are responsible to give their children principles that will guide their entire lives.

> ## WHAT KINDS OF CHARACTERISTICS AND VALUES DO YOU HOPE TO PASS ON TO YOUR CHILDREN?
>
> _____
>
> _____
>
> _____
>
> _____
>
> _____

Discipline

Rules usually don't carry much weight unless there are consequences for breaking them. Just as parents have responsibility to make rules that guide us, they are also responsible to make sure we follow them. If there is disobedience, discipline must follow. Without it, chaos will ensue. And no parent wants that for his or her child. Proverbs 3:12 tells us, "The LORD corrects those he loves, just as parents correct the child they delight in." In Hebrews 12:8–11, we see a fuller picture of the purpose and importance of discipline:

> If you are never disciplined (and every child must be disciplined), you are not true children. We have all had fathers here on earth who disciplined us, and we respected them. So it is even more important that we accept discipline from the Father of our spirits so we will have life. Our fathers on earth disciplined us for a short time in the way they thought was best.

But God disciplines us to help us, so we can become holy as he is. We do not enjoy being disciplined. It is painful, but later, after we have learned from it, we have peace, because we start living in the right way.

Again, God provides a model of what it means to be a parent and how children should respond.

OUR RESPONSIBILITY

Compared to the responsibilities that our parents have to God, believe it or not, children have it pretty easy. We've looked a bit at parents' responsibilities, but let's get back to our rule. "Honor your father and your mother." *Honor.* What does it mean? According to *Strong's Concordance,* the word *honor* that is used in our rule means "to make weighty." No, it doesn't mean to make them "fat and heavy," but to treat them as seriously important (as in the opposite of "taking them lightly"). And important they are. They are the people who hold our futures in their hands. We are called to respect them and their decisions. And we are called to obey them.

HOW OFTEN DO YOU DISAGREE WITH YOUR PARENTS?

Colossians 3:20 says, "Children, obey your parents in all things, because this pleases the Lord." Because parents love us,

they make rules that let us know the best way to live. Think back to the first commandment, in which God reminded us that He is our Creator. Because He created us, loves us, and wants the very best for us, He has the right and authority to give us rules and instruction that we are expected to follow and obey. The same is true for parents.

If you have recently had a conflict with your parents, you may be thinking to yourself, *Hey, well at least this rule doesn't say that I have to* love *them.* Buzzer sound: Wrong. That is the one rule that goes hand in hand with all commands ever given by God. If you remember from our first rule, we are to love God, even when we don't feel like it. Likewise, we are to commit to choose to love our parents always—even when we don't agree with them or think they have lost their minds. Honor and love of our parents don't have a time limit either. Yes, even when we turn eighteen, leave home for college, move away for a new job, get married, and have children of our own, we are never to stop giving honor or love to our parents.

Proverbs 23:22 commands, "Listen to your father, who gave you life, and do not forget your mother when she is old." And in 1 Timothy 5:8, after advising how to treat widows, Paul says, "Whoever does not care for his own relatives, especially his own family members, has turned against the faith and is worse than someone who does not believe in God." So we are to listen and learn, honor and obey, and always love. This is what God expects from us as our parents' children.

ALL AUTHORITY

Now, I realize that this whole chapter might be very painful for some. Some of us might not be living in what was once considered a typical American family. We might be living with only one parent or away from both of our birth parents in an adoptive family, in foster care, or possibly even as a ward of the state. Or we might have very difficult experiences with the parents we do live with. No matter our current situation, painful or pleasant, this rule applies to us.

First, we'll note that while God gave this rule as specific to parents (or guardians) because those are the first people we are to learn from, honor, and obey, in general this rule covers all in authority at any given time. The Bible is clear that we are to honor all those in authority, whether it be a boss, the government, or the church. Hebrews 13:17 says, "Obey your leaders and act under their authority. They are watching over you, because they are responsible for your souls. Obey them so that they will do this work with joy, not sadness. It will not help you to make their work hard." Young or old, powerful or weak, we all are under the authority of someone else, and that someone else is under the authority of someone else, and ultimately, we are all under God's authority.

WHO ARE THE PEOPLE IN AUTHORITY OVER YOU?

_____

_____

_____

In Romans 13:1 we read, "All of you must yield to the government rulers. No one rules unless God has given him the power to rule, and no one rules now without that power from God." God, in His divine wisdom, created this world with a certain hierarchy in place, and this rule has everything to do with that. Yes, we are to honor our parents, whether birth parents, adoptive parents, or any other person who cares for and guides us. We are to honor all in authority.

IMPERFECT PARENTS

While we've talked a lot about the parallel between parents' relationships with their children and God's relationship with humankind, there is a significant difference to keep in mind. Our parents are not perfect, and they are not God. They happen to be sinners just like us. So now what do we do? Are they to be trusted? God knows that our parents are imperfect sinners, but He has still given them this place in our lives. We are to trust in God's decision to provide these parents for us, remember that they are responsible to Him for their actions, and rest in God's being the ultimate Father and authority.

Limits

As we have seen, by honoring and loving our parents we are loving God. God has advanced them to the place they have over us. Now comes another hard question. One or both of our parents or guardians may not be followers of Jesus or followers of God's laws. They might even be against the things of God and get excited about doing wrong and sinful things. What if our parents ask us or expect us to live in a way that goes directly against God and His rules? What are we to do? We must choose God's way rather than the way of our parents.

Ephesians 6:1 says, "Children, obey your parents *as the Lord wants,* because this is the right thing to do" (emphasis added). God appoints our parents to their positions and allows them to share a part of His honor. Therefore, honoring our parents is a step toward honoring our Father in heaven. But if our parents urge us to break God's rules, we have the right to view them as people trying to lure us away from obeying our one true Father and into enemy hands. Earthly authority should never grow so great that it replaces or tears down God's authority. On the contrary, earthly authority depends on God's absolute authority and ought to lead us to it.[1] As followers of Jesus, we also have the responsibility to lead others, even our own parents, by our example. If you are a living example of the goodness of God, your life might be the very thing that leads your parents into the truth of God. But again, if you are left with a choice between following God's rules or following your parents in something that leads you away from God, it is right to follow God's way.

Be very careful with this idea and in these situations. You must be certain of God's law and use that as a measure against what your parents ask of you. It would be wise to seek the counsel of a pastor or other spiritual leader if you find yourself battling between following God and following your parents.

GIVE AN EXAMPLE OF SOMETHING YOUR PARENTS MIGHT ASK YOU TO DO THAT WOULD BE AGAINST GOD.

_____

_____

_____

_____

_____

---

1. (Calvin, John. *Institutes of the Christian Religion*, 2.8.38.)

Also, this does *not* mean that you are ever excused from your duty to love your parents. If your parents are not practicing Christians, this does not mean that you can or should live at odds with them. God tells us how to live in Ephesians 5:1–2, saying, "You are God's children whom he loves, so try to be like him. Live a life of love just as Christ loved us and gave himself for us as a sweet-smelling offering and sacrifice to God." And really, if you think about it, what better way is there to honor someone, or to let them know their importance, than to live in such a way that they will see Christ and know His love.

THE PROMISE

The last part of our rule says that it is to be followed "so that you will live a long time in the land that the LORD your God is going to give you." Ephesians 6:2 points out that this is the first and only command that has a promise with it. God has set up the parent-child relationship for a reason. God intends for us to learn His ways and hear His instructions through our parents. His instructions lead us into a life of freedom and prosperity. Psalm 1:1-2 tells us that those who love and dwell on the Lord's teachings are happy people.

CONCLUSION

Will you honor your parents and all that means? What are some specific ways you can choose to love and honor your parents, even in difficult situations?

Let's thank God for loving us so much that He surrounds us with tangible examples of His love here on earth as we receive food, shelter, knowledge, and instruction from our parents and others in authority.

FIVE WAYS I WILL CHOOSE TO LOVE AND HONOR MY PARENTS ARE:

1. _____

2. _____

3. _____

4. _____

5. _____

MURDER

You must not murder anyone.

(Exodus 20:13)

As far as rules go, this appears to be the granddaddy of them all. The biggest, baddest, most ominous rule of them all, but thankfully, it seems to be the easiest to follow. You shall not kill or murder anyone. Have you ever murdered anyone? No? I haven't either. So that's the end of this chapter, right? Well, before we jump ahead, let's take a closer look at this rule, see why it is such a big deal, and take an honest look at our hearts and lives to see if we've ever come close to breaking this rule.

WORKING TOGETHER

God cares for living things. He created living things, and He sustains living things. This includes plants, animals of every kind, and of course, human beings, whom He created in His own image. Even after sin and death entered the world, God maintained a balance and cycle of life that continue to this day. To get a better idea of how God makes everything work together, let's check out Psalm 104:10–33:

HOW ARE YOU CREATED IN GOD'S IMAGE?

_____

_____

_____

_____

You make springs pour into the ravines;
    they flow between the mountains.
They water all the wild animals;
    the wild donkeys come there to drink.
Wild birds make nests by the water;
    they sing among the tree branches.
You water the mountains from above.
    The earth is full of the things you made.
You make the grass for cattle
    and vegetables for the people.
    You make food grow from the earth.
You give us wine that makes happy hearts
    and olive oil that makes our faces shine.
    You give us bread that gives us strength.
The LORD's trees have plenty of water;
    they are the cedars of Lebanon, which he planted.
The birds make their nests there;
    the stork's home is in the fir trees.
The high mountains belong to the wild goats.
    The rocks are hiding places for the badgers.

You made the moon to mark the seasons,
    and the sun always knows when to set.
You make it dark, and it becomes night.
    Then all the wild animals creep around.
The lions roar as they attack.
    They look to God for food.
When the sun rises, they leave
    and go back to their dens to lie down.
Then people go to work
    and work until evening.

LORD, you have made many things;
    with your wisdom you made them all.

The earth is full of your riches.
Look at the sea so big and wide,
>   with creatures large and small that cannot be counted.
Ships travel over the ocean,
>   and there is the sea monster Leviathan,
>   which you made to play there.

All these things depend on you
>   to give them their food at the right time.
When you give it to them,
>   they gather it up.
When you open your hand,
>   they are filled with good food.
When you turn away from them,
>   they become frightened.
When you take away their breath,
>   they die and turn to dust.
When you breathe on them,
>   they are created,
>   and you make the land new again.

May the glory of the LORD be forever.
>   May the LORD enjoy what he has made.
He just looks at the earth, and it shakes.
>   He touches the mountains, and they smoke.

I will sing to the LORD all my life;
>   I will sing praises to my God as long as I live.

What a great picture of God's sustaining love for all His creation! And it is not just about *human*kind's life that God is concerned. He makes sure that the birds will have a home. He cares for the grass so that livestock have something to eat. He cares for vegetables so that people have things to eat as well. God has purpose for all living things, and they play a specific part in His plan for this world. Since God is both Creator and Sustainer of all living things, it makes sense that God also has the ultimate say over life and death.

But God did give us some responsibility when it comes to living things. He tells us how we are to handle life and what we can and cannot do.

In Genesis 9:3–6, God says,

> Everything that moves, everything that is alive, is yours for food. Earlier I gave you the green plants, but now I give you everything for food. But you must not eat meat that still has blood in it, because blood gives life. I will demand blood for life. I will demand the life of any animal that kills a person, and I will demand the life of anyone who takes another person's life.
>
> Whoever kills a human being
>   will be killed by a human being,
> because God made humans
>   in his own image.

In Scripture, God does two things. One, He tells us that it is okay to eat meat. In effect, God gives us authority over the lives of animals in order that we may feed ourselves. We have not murdered if we eat a hamburger. But then He goes on to put the highest premium that could possibly exist on human life: Take another person's life and your life will be taken away. God even gave us the reason for such a serious punishment: God made us all in His image. We bear a resemblance to God Himself, and to kill a person is to permanently erase that image of God from this earth. We would be taking matters into our own hands.

The giving and taking of a human being's life is reserved for only God Himself; therefore, we have rule six: You must not murder anyone. This is easy to agree to in principle, but it seems there are a good number of scenarios that might not always be so clear-cut.

ARE YOU A VEGETARIAN?

WAR

The first situation to come up always seems to be: Is it okay to kill people during times of war? This is a good question. Some translations of the Bible refer to murder as "unlawful killing," inferring that there is a place for lawful killing, as in times of war.

The word that God uses in this rule is the Hebrew word *ratsach*, which means simply "to murder or put to death." It implies an act of hostility, passion, and unlawful behavior. But God makes a distinction in His Word for times in which His people must go to war. For example, in Deuteronomy 20:13 as God is giving His people rules for war, He instructs them to "kill all the men with your swords" (but not to kill the women, children, or animals). The word God uses for *kill* is the Hebrew word *nakah*, which means "to strike with the intent to harm or kill." This word carries the implication of punishment. But God does not put the responsibility for punishment or killing in times of war in the hands of you and me; God puts that burden on the shoulders of the government. However, in our country we have a government that allows the citizens to have a voice in the decisions our leaders make. This means that we as followers of God have a responsibility to help our government make wise decisions about things like war. If you believe our government isn't handling matters of life and death in accordance with God's rules, speak up and let your voice be heard.

In Scripture, God establishes with governments "the power of the sword" or "the power to punish" in order to uphold goodness and destroy evil. In Romans 13:4 God tells us: "The ruler is God's servant to help you. But if you do wrong, then be afraid. He has the power to punish; he is God's servant to punish those who do wrong."

If we are called to war, our government calls us to the act of doing battle, even to the point of taking another human life. There is a big difference between unlawful killing (read *murder*) and killing in times of war, and God places responsibility on the government to act in a way that is in keeping with God's law when it comes to enforcing justice, freedom, and peace.

> **DO YOU THINK IT'S OKAY TO KILL SOMEONE IN BATTLE?**
>
> _____
>
> _____
>
> _____

SELF-DEFENSE

What then about self-defense? Another very good question. After all, if someone is trying to rob or even murder you, they are obviously acting in an extremely unlawful way. So the question is: Is it okay to stop someone from acting against you, to the point of killing that person? Well, first we must remember again that God is the Creator and Sustainer of all life, that He loves life and is in the very business of life-giving, and we should be too. With that in mind, let's look at Exodus 22:2–4 and see what answers God provides us for this question:

> If a thief is killed while breaking into a house at night, the one who killed him is not guilty of murder. But if this happens during the day, he is guilty of murder.

TO WHAT EXTENT IS SELF-DEFENSE ACCEPTABLE?

_____

_____

_____

_____

_____

Now this seems perplexing. Why would a homeowner be guilty of a robber's death during the daytime but not at night? Let's think about the two scenarios in greater detail. At night, if there were an intruder in our house, we couldn't see very well, or think very clearly, especially if we had just been awakened from our sleep. If a struggle or fight broke out in the darkness, you would be less able to protect both yourself and the intruder, and it could cost the intruder his life. But by the light of day, we are expected to be able to preserve both our life and the life of the intruder, while combating his evil intentions. We are never to be in a position in which we purposely try to kill anyone, even the vilest of criminals entering our homes to do us harm. It seems that this Scripture does make way for the exception of the accidental death of an intruder while we are defending self and home, yet everything possible must be done to protect the intruder's life. This would seem to be in keeping with our life-loving God.

Since the next two issues are painful, emotional, and complex issues, much could be said about them. However, at this time, I am just going to explore briefly how they relate to the sixth commandment and bring some Scripture to bear on them.

ABORTION

Much of the debate about abortion comes down to one question: When does human life begin? Those who are in favor of abortion assert that life begins at some point during a woman's pregnancy, usually between six and nine months, the point at which a baby can reasonably survive outside the mother's womb. Most others who are decidedly against abortion would agree that human life begins at conception—the moment the sperm enters the egg and starts the process of cell division. Let's look at what the Bible has to say about the unborn:

> You made my whole being;
>> you formed me in my mother's body.
> I praise you because you made me in an amazing and wonderful way.
>> What you have done is wonderful.
>> I know this very well.
> You saw my bones being formed
>> as I took shape in my mother's body.
> When I was put together there,
>> you saw my body as it was formed.
> All the days planned for me
>> were written in your book
>> before I was one day old. (Psalm 139:13–16)

Your hands shaped and made me.
>Do you now turn around and destroy me?
Remember that you molded me like a piece of clay.
>Will you now turn me back into dust?
You formed me inside my mother
>like cheese formed from milk.
You dressed me with skin and flesh;
>you sewed me together with bones and muscles.
You gave me life and showed me kindness,
>and in your care you watched over my life. (Job 10:8–12)

When Elizabeth heard Mary's greeting, the unborn baby inside her jumped, and Elizabeth was filled with the Holy Spirit. . . . "When I heard your voice, the baby inside me jumped with joy." (Luke 1:41, 44)

From the sound of all three of these passages, it is apparent that God Himself has a direct hand in the creation and growth of the unborn. We also know He cares deeply about His creation, particularly humans who are made in His image. It follows that He would not want us to terminate human life that He has created, either inside or outside the womb. It is also important to remember that God calls us to trust in His authority, sovereignty, and power to provide for those He has created and loves.

Abortion is a messy topic and should be handled with great care. If you know anyone who has terminated the life of an unborn child, or who is considering taking such action, it would be in his or her best interest for you to show them the love and compassion that come from Christ. Christ didn't come with anger and judgment to those who were hurting, like the prostitutes or the outcasts of society, He came with loving-kindness. Since abortion involves such intense situations and emotions, in dealing with others on this topic the best practice is to "let your kindness and gentleness be evident to all" (Philippians 4:5).

WHAT IS YOUR STANCE ON THE ABORTION ISSUE?

_____

_____

_____

_____

SUICIDE

I have personally known or been acquainted with four people who chose to end their lives by suicide. (I also know several more who have tried and, thankfully, failed.) Each of them had a profoundly sad and disturbing story. Like those I've known, thoughts of suicide can stem from physiological disorders such as mental illness and chronic depression, as well as other factors contributing to a sense of hopelessness, such as divorce, abuse, and alcoholism. Counselors have also found that suicidal people are often angry and use their own murder to inflict pain or retribution on others. With suicide being the third leading cause of death among people ages ten to twenty-four, and nine percent of those in that age group attempting suicide in 2001, it is likely you have known or will know someone in this situation.[1]

With all the violence, abuse, and chaos in today's world, it can be easy to fall into hopelessness, anger, and despair. Is this

---

1. http://www.cdc.gov/nccdphp/dash/yrbs/2001/summary_results/usa.htm.

phenomenon unique to our generation? The Bible is full of stories of people who underwent intense suffering for long periods,
accompanied by serious doubt about their value and even about
God's love. Look at the story of Job, or at some of David's
psalms. In Psalm 22:1, David says, "My God, My God, why
have You forsaken Me? Why are You so far from helping Me,
and from the words of My groaning?" (NKJV). It's important to
remember, though, that the Bible is also full of reprieve, healing,
redemption, and great blessing for these people as well. Look at
the Israelites, who were freed from slavery in Egypt, or the man
Jesus healed who had been sick and unable to walk for thirty-
eight years. The story God lays out for His people, including
you and me, is usually much more amazing and grand than we
can imagine.

DO YOU THINK SUICIDE IS A VIABLE OPTION FOR ELIMINATING PAIN?

Let's also look at the story of a man who came very close to
killing himself. Acts 16:23–34 tells the story of a jailer who was
ordered to guard Paul and Silas in prison. In the middle of the
night, an earthquake caused the doors of the jail and the chains
on the prisoners to break open. When the jailer awoke and saw
this, he assumed the prisoners had escaped, and he knew his
boss would kill him for allowing this to happen. Facing what
was an overwhelming and apparently hopeless situation, the
jailer got out his sword. As he prepared to kill himself, he was
interrupted by a shout from Paul: "Don't hurt yourself! We are

all here" (v. 28). When the jailer saw that the prisoners were still there, he was in awe, as what had seemed unfathomable was indeed true. As he spoke with Paul and Silas, the jailer heard the message of Jesus' salvation and believed. As he was pulling out his sword, the jailer did not imagine that God had planned for him not only delivery from punishment but also eternal life.

What are we to think of people who want to or have taken their own lives? We should be filled with compassion and sorrow that a life should end in such a devastating way. We can love people through the darkness of their despair, offering prayer and friendship and leading them to professional care or help. Most important, we should know that God is powerful through suffering, doubt, anger, and even death. In Hebrews 4:15*a*, 16, we are reminded, "For our high priest [Jesus] is able to understand our weaknesses. . . . Let us, then, feel very sure that we can come before God's throne where there is grace. There we can receive mercy and grace to help us when we need it."

JESUS' DEFINITION

So, what if you've never physically killed someone, gone to war, or encountered someone who's dealt with abortion or suicide? Does the command not to murder have anything to do with you? Let's look at what Jesus says in Matthew 5:21–22:

> You have heard that it was said to our people long ago, "You must not murder anyone. Anyone who murders another will be judged." But I tell you, if you are angry with a brother or sister, you will be judged. If you say bad things to a brother or sister, you will be judged by the council. And if you call someone a fool, you will be in danger of the fire of hell.

I don't know anyone who isn't guilty of at least one of these things. In fact, most of us are guilty of them every day. Jesus gives us this instruction for two reasons. One, He is giving us a full definition of *murder*—in thought, word, and deed. Two, these words expose our great need for Him. At first look, we might think we can easily keep the sixth commandment. However, using Jesus' definition, none of us on our own will obey to the extent that is truly required. Jesus is the only One who fulfills the law. And it is His righteousness that saves us.

FAR FROM HOME

Now let's look at one more aspect of this rule, which may seem unrelated. In the time it just took me to type that sentence, one person in Africa died of AIDS. If you have sat down and read this book straight through, about 370 people have died of AIDS since you started. There is an AIDS emergency in Africa, with millions of our neighbors dying every year—many of them children. There are twelve million AIDS orphans in Africa. These are staggering numbers. But more than numbers, they are people, God's creation, with real faces, hearts, pains, and dreams.

IS IGNORING PEOPLE IN THEIR NEED MURDER?

We in America have the drugs, which, for less than a dollar, can save the lives of children born to HIV positive mothers. Drugs which can extend the lives of children and adults currently living with HIV/AIDS. What are we doing about it? Has your

1. The statistics are constantly changing. For up-to-date information go to www.unaids.org.

church become involved in helping with this emergency? You can talk to church leaders, pray, and donate time and money. You can even call the White House and ask the president to direct more money to medicine and education for these people.

All around the world, and even in your hometown, people are hurting and dying from things like hunger, homelessness, and disease. Are you sitting idly by, or are you living out God's love to them and helping to preserve life?

CONCLUSION

Knowing that killing and murder are so ultimately offensive to God, it is mind-blowing to remember that God allowed Jesus (God in human form) to be murdered as a payment for the curse of sin. It is even cooler to remember that God proved Himself to be more powerful than death and that He triumphed over it.

Whether through movies, TV, music, video games, or people we know, we are being told in some subtle and some not so subtle ways that life is less valuable than it truly is. But we serve a God who is the Creator and Sustainer of life. Jesus tells us, "I came to give life—life in all its fullness" (John 10:10).

FIVE THINGS I WILL DO TO STOP PATTERNS OF MURDER IN MY LIFE:

1. _____

2. _____

3. _____

4. _____

5. _____

HOOKIN' UP

RULE #7

You must not be guilty of adultery.
(Exodus 20:14)

If you are not currently married and having sex with someone who is not your spouse, does this rule apply to you? Yes. How and why? Let's take a few steps back and look at what it's all about.

> **a*dul*ter*y,** n.—voluntary sexual intercourse between a married person and someone other than his or her lawful spouse. *(Random House Webster's College Dictionary)*

WHAT'S IT FOR?

Sex. There is not a more provocative topic than sex. It is whispered about in secret, and it is splayed across the headlines of newspapers. Movies are made about it, songs are sung about it, books and magazines on the subject are bestsellers. Some people make their living by engaging in it, and other people sell their products by using it in their advertising. Some of our most popular TV shows (and even entire TV channels) are dedicated to sex. It is everywhere, all around us. For some people, it's all they want to talk about, and on the other hand, there are a lot of Christians who shy away from the topic altogether. So what did God have in mind when He created man and woman with the ability and desire to have sex?

God's intent was not to create something taboo (not ever talked about) or something so common it would be seen on billboards. No, God created the sexual encounter to be the most personal act of a human being's love and service toward another in an atmosphere of trust. This being so, it was designed so that each person would share and experience it with only *one* other person—husband or wife—during life here on earth.

The marriage relationship between men and women bears a striking parallel to our relationship with God. Jesus refers to Himself as the bridegroom in Matthew 9:15. In Revelation 21:9–10, God's people are described as the bride. God's design for sexual intercourse within marriage points to the closeness and intimacy we were created to have with God—where we come as we are, fully exposed and unashamed before God, to serve, enjoy, and be fully loved by Him.

The marriage covenant between two people is like God's covenant of salvation with us, meant to be constant, unbroken, and full of mercy and grace. It's pretty cool that God would give us something as tangible as marriage to show us, albeit in smaller and imperfect ways, how rewarding and fulfilling our relationship with Him can be.

THE ME FACTOR

All relationships, particularly marriage, are priceless and should be treasured and protected at all costs. God designed human beings with a need for relationship and intimacy. That is why God created both Adam and Eve, so they would fulfill those needs in each other. Before sin entered the picture, Adam, Eve, and God together completed the relationship and intimacy picture quite nicely. But sin, of course, messed that up quite a bit. Sin made all humankind ask the question "What about me?"

Asking this question is where adultery begins. Self-centeredness will try to break in and destroy relationships of any kind whether it be marriage, a dating relationship, or friendship. If you put yourself ahead of your partner or think you're the more important person, your relationship is headed for a rough time. Philippians 2:3–4 tells us, "When you do things, do not let selfishness or pride be your guide. Instead, be humble and give more honor to others than to yourselves. Do not be interested only in your own life, but be interested in the lives of others."

Relationships are the messiest and yet the most rewarding of gifts God gives us. There are hundreds of factors that can cause someone to start looking out for themselves first, like betrayed trust, physical abuse, emotional distance, or lust. When intimacy or trust is betrayed, it is normal to retreat from the betrayer so you will not get hurt. But since God makes us to need relationship and intimacy, we will go out looking for it somewhere else. If you are in a covenant relationship like marriage, looking for intimacy outside God and your spouse, whether emotionally or physically, is wrong. It is adultery.

WHAT ELSE DO YOU CONSIDER ADULTERY?

I have witnessed many marriages collapse for varied reasons, and each time it is a profoundly sad occasion. But each case always involves selfishness and unfaithfulness. Whether or not that unfaithfulness ends up in the act of sex, it is still adultery. Adultery of any kind is destructive in a marriage. It has devastating effects on both the spouses and the children left behind. If you are part of a family that has been broken by divorce due to adultery, you probably have firsthand knowledge of this pain, heartache, and turmoil.

If we properly recognize that our spouses have been provided for us, in the exact same way God provided Adam and Eve for each other, any break in the marriage covenant through adultery is a sin against God. By nature, the act of adultery is telling God the person He has provided for you as a partner is worthless and He is worthless for giving such a gift. It is an act of hostility and outright rebellion against God. It is a rejection of His plan and the good gifts He has given.

At this point in your reading, you might be screaming in your head, *But I'm not married and this has nothing to do with how I live my life right now!* Let's look at how this rule about adultery applies to everyone, including you.

FORNICATORS

Our dictionary definition of *adultery* at the beginning of the chapter talks about a married person's having sex with someone other than their lawful spouse. But what about sex outside marriage between two unattached people? If you are unmarried and have sex with someone else who is unmarried, is that person your lawful spouse? No. Even if you think you might marry or are engaged to that other person? No. You would still be having sex with someone who is not your "lawful spouse." You would be, in fact, committing adultery, but there is another word in the Bible that more clearly defines sex outside marriage: fornication.

Since we've seen that God designed sex to be enjoyed solely within the context of marriage, it follows then that sex between unmarried people, or fornication, is not a part of His plan for us either. The reasons for this again have to do with what is in our best interests. The consequences of sex outside marriage can be very difficult. There are emotional stresses like feelings of guilt, fear, and emptiness, as well as the potential physical results of disease or a pregnancy that you're not ready for.

WHAT SITUATIONS MAKE YOU FEEL MORE SEXUALLY TEMPTED?

_____

_____

_____

_____

_____

The Bible tells us we are to honor God with our bodies and stay away from sexual sin. First Corinthians 6:19–20 says, "You should know that your body is a temple for the Holy Spirit who is in you. You have received the Holy Spirit from God. So you do not belong to yourselves, because you were bought by God for a price. So honor God with your bodies." And we learn in 1 Thessalonians 4:3–6, "God wants you to be holy and to stay away from sexual sins. He wants each of you to learn to control your own body in a way that is holy and honorable. Don't use your body for sexual sin like the people who do not know God. . . . The Lord will punish people who do those things as we have already told you and warned you."

I had a friend in my church youth group who was quite proud of his virginity. He was also pleased that he was following Scripture, though he would participate in virtually all sexual activity up to the point of having actual sexual intercourse. In his words, he was just "running the bases." Was he really honoring God with his body and treating it like a temple for the Holy Spirit? Was he even cheating others out of their innocence and out of experiences that were really meant to be shared with their future husbands?

There are probably plenty of people who would like to argue that a little bit of light sexual contact that doesn't include actual intercourse is okay. But is it?

In chapter 3, verse 5 of the poetic Song of Solomon, we read the words: "Women of Jerusalem, promise me by the gazelles and the deer not to awaken or excite my feelings of love until it is ready." We should all be careful not to excite our desires until it is time; and the time for sex of any kind is marriage. We must be careful even when kissing another person outside of marriage, because it has the rampant tendency to escalate into a sexually charged situation that will lead to the breaking of this rule.

Making out is like playing with fire. The Bible acknowledges the reality of sexual temptation among unmarried people. Paul says in 1 Corinthians 7:9, "But if they cannot control themselves, they should marry. It is better to marry than to burn with sexual desire." Physical intimacy comes only with the promise and commitment of marriage, and we are never to make promises that we cannot keep. Remember, we are to honor God proactively with our bodies, not just avoid getting into trouble.

So, what if you've never even come close to having sex and don't plan on it until you are married? Does this rule have anything to say to you right now? Well, let's look at Jesus' words

WHAT'S YOUR MOTIVATION TO STAY PURE?

on the subject. You may remember from the last chapter that Jesus gave us a deeper definition of murder that included more than just our physical acts. Similarly, Jesus says, "You have heard that it was said, 'You must not be guilty of adultery.' But I tell you that if anyone looks at a woman and wants to sin sexually with her, in his mind he has already done that sin with the woman" (Matthew 5:27–28). We are supposed to honor God with our thoughts as well as our actions. For this reason, we should avoid things like pornography, strip clubs, or even dressing in ways that might cause someone to lust. We know from experience, and we see it confirmed in Galatians 5:17, that our sinful selves will naturally want what is against the Spirit. As we rely on God's Spirit to work in us and change our hearts, we should steer clear of situations that would cause us to sin in our thoughts or actions.

RESPONSIBILITY

When it comes to sex, we have a responsibility not only to ourselves but also to others to help keep them pure as well.

Guys! I know what goes on with you because I'm a guy and

I go through it all too. Most often, we struggle with what we see. For whatever reason, God made us very sight-oriented. We see things all the time that get into our brains and refuse to leave. Whether it is a pretty girl who smiles in our direction, a billboard over the interstate depicting a beautiful woman in a tight dress trying to sell us cell phones, or typing in the wrong Web address and being confronted with porn, once we see things, they get stuck in our heads, and we have a tendency to let our imaginations take over from there. When we let our imaginations take over sexually and we lust in our hearts, we break this rule.

If you are in a dating relationship or courtship, you must be quite careful how you handle yourself. Guys learn to be convincing and manipulative with their girlfriends if they find themselves aroused. Once your hormones start racing around, you have only one thing on your mind. You can become quite opportunistic and convince your girlfriend to participate in things that she (and you) should not. It is at times like these when guys are the most self-centered. You are responsible to set up safe rules that will keep both yourself and your girlfriend out of any situation that could lead to breaking this rule.

ARE GIRLS RESPONSIBLE FOR THE WAY GUYS THINK ABOUT THEM?

Girls! You might be thinking this is more a guy's problem than yours. Guys are the ones who are always whistling at you from across the mall, staring at your figure, or being "Mr. Grabby Hands" when you're on dates with them. This is a two-way street though. While girls are certainly not without the ability to notice a guy's appearance, they tend to be more motivated by a desire for emotional intimacy—to know and be known. Girls generally want relationships in which they will be respected, loved, and taken care of. But how is it that you get a guy to notice you in the first place so that you can have that relationship? Usually by your appearance. Making yourself attractive is not a bad thing in and of itself. Just be aware of what kind of image you are portraying, though, and what kind of thoughts you might be stirring up in a guy's mind. Girls, you have a responsibility to love and care for guys by not flaunting your bodies in tight or revealing clothes. And be careful not to let your desire for intimacy drive you to do things that will leave you feeling empty if experienced outside the bond of marriage.

As you're working through your relationships, listen to God's Word found in 2 Timothy 2:22: "But run away from the evil young people like to do. Try hard to live right and to have faith, love, and peace, together with those who trust in the Lord from pure hearts."

WHAT ABOUT HOMOSEXUALITY?

God's Word is clear that homosexuality does not fall under His intention for our romantic lives. Romans 1:24-26 describes women having sex with women and men having sex with men as "sinful" and "using their bodies wrongly with each other." Just as sinful hearts cause unmarried heterosexuals to desire and give in to having sex with each other, it is also because of sin that others desire people of their same sex. It is all a departure from

God's perfect plan for sexual intimacy to be reserved for marriage between a man and a woman.

I am sure that you, like me, have people in your life who struggle with homosexuality. I have friends who have wrestled with this sin and found what I believe is complete healing in the arms of a merciful God. I have other friends who have given up their struggle and given in to this lifestyle. I also have several friends who have submitted their lives to God and know Jesus to be their Savior and Redeemer but they still wrestle daily with desire for those of the same sex. For these friends are faith, salvation and love of Christ any less alive? Not at all. Is this normal? Quite.

Just because someone commits himself or herself to Christ, it doesn't necessarily mean that all temptation and wrong desires disappear. Romans 7:21-25 makes it clear that we will always wrestle with temptation and the desire not to follow God's rules. The Christian life is not an escape from temptation but the ability to lean heavily into God's grace and learn to deal with temptation the way Christ would have. This is true not only for those who struggle with homosexual desires but for those with wrong heterosexual desires, those who lie, those who steal, those who idolize, covet, etc. It is true for us all.

WHAT IS YOUR ATTITUDE TOWARD THE HOMOSEXUAL COMMUNITY?

While the homosexual lifestyle is clearly not part of God's plan for His people and cannot be justified by using Scripture, there is a great tragedy that has taken place that centers on this very issue. The tragedy has been the church's response to those who struggle with this particular sin. I should have said "lack of response," because more often than not the church has either ignored or shamed these people and left them to deal with their brokenness alone.

Many churches shut their doors to the homosexual community. This is so amazingly contrary to the teachings and life of Jesus that it blows my mind! Jesus chose to hang out with drunkards, thieves, and, yes, even prostitutes, who made their livings from sexual sin. Jesus loved these people unconditionally and so should we. In Matthew 9:11-12, the Pharisees ask why Jesus eats with tax collectors and sinners. "When Jesus heard them, he said, 'It is not the healthy people who need a doctor, but the sick.'" Jesus came not for the perfect and blameless (of which there are none) but for the broken and needy. He came for the rule breakers. He came for you and me. And this certainly includes anyone who struggles with homosexuality.

If we find ourselves wanting to shun or turn our back on anyone, we must remember that we are no better than anyone else. The Bible tells us, "All have sinned and are not good enough for God's glory, and all need to be made right with God by his grace, which is a free gift. They need to be made free from sin through Jesus Christ" (Romans 3:23-24).

THE "M" WORD

Here comes a word that's sure to get your attention: *masturbation*. It doesn't matter whether you are a guy or a girl, old or young, the word masturbation inevitably evokes a strong reaction in people. This could possibly be one of the most secretive, shameful, and embarrassing topics that there is. But let's get past the awkwardness for a moment and get right down to the heart of this subject.

God created us as sexual beings. This is a good thing, a thing that God is not shy about. God created our sexual impulses for good and they are quite normal and natural. These are not urges we are to be ashamed of, nor are we to act as though they don't exist.

As we discussed earlier, God created sex to be a beautiful act of intimacy between a husband and wife, an act that is enjoyable and the only natural way possible for people to reproduce and have children. God even designed male and female bodies so that they are sexually compatible, and it is obvious that His design for sex is to be a mutual act and not for that of an individual.

Masturbation is not God's original plan for sexuality. This more than anything is the probably the best argument against masturbation. Masturbation not only falls far short of the great gift that God created sex to be, but it's often the result of thoughts and feelings that are not right either. The road to masturbation usually begins in the mind with the imagination. Feeding your mind with images and thoughts that are sexually provocative must be avoided at all costs. Pornography is the most obvious example and is lurking everywhere you turn, but I can name dozens of beer commercials, music videos, hip-hop songs, and even books that contain images or ideas that are sexually provocative.

We should always be on guard and careful with the things we allow into our minds, because if we start fixating on those things they can lead to covetousness, lust, and idolatry. There are other things like loneliness and even boredom that can also factor in to the desire to masturbate. The act of masturbation is in essence a person trying to fix or repair something that God alone can fix.

If this is a struggle for you, the first thing to do is look to the One who is able to help you through the things that do need fixing in your life. Commit your sexuality to God and surrender this aspect of your life to Him. Ask Him to help you through those things that might lead you to less than God's very best plan for your life.

Remember that God gave you your sexuality as a gift and it is quite appropriate to seek His help in understanding and dealing with sexual things. God does not want us to be enslaved by anything. He wants us to be free: free to enjoy the life He created us to live and not tangled up in cycle of useless behavior.

CONCLUSION

Whether it's a woman who cheated on her husband, a guy who wants to sleep with his girlfriend, a teenager struggling with an attraction to someone of the same sex, or someone's attempt to satisfy themselves through masturbation, all are in need of Jesus' grace and forgiveness. We should agree with the words of Paul in 1 Timothy 1:15–17:

> What I say is true, and you should fully accept it: Christ Jesus came into the world to save sinners, of whom I am the worst. But I was given mercy so that in me, the worst of all sinners, Christ Jesus could show that he has patience without limit. His patience with me made me an example for those who would believe in him and have life forever. To the King that rules forever, who will never die, who cannot be seen, the only God, be honor and glory forever and ever. Amen.

Let's thank God for His unending mercy and for the gift of sexuality. And let's recognize His authority and goodness, using His gifts only in the relationships for which they were intended, as we anticipate the "wedding of the Lamb" (Revelation 19:7), in which we'll experience a greater pleasure and intimacy than anything we could imagine here on earth.

> Dear friends, you are like foreigners and strangers in this world. I beg you to avoid the evil things your bodies want to do that fight against your soul. People who do not believe are living all around you and might say that you are doing wrong. Live such good lives that they will see the good things you do and will give glory to God on the day when Christ comes again. (1 Peter 2:11–12)

FIVE WAYS I'LL CHANGE MY HABITS TO AVOID ADULTERY ARE:

1. _____

2. _____

3. _____

4. _____

5. _____

FIVE-FINGER DISCOUNT

RULE #8

You must not steal.

(Exodus 20:15)

I will never forget the day. The skies were gray and the wind was cutting through the leafless branches and making whips out of the twigs. I was three, maybe four years old, and I was on a mission with my mom. She had a big project to do, and we were on our way to shop for supplies from the fabric store. There was a sense of great importance about what we were doing, and I recall that I too felt important and all grown up. I could sense that ours was a mission of significance, but only later would I understand how significant that day was to become.

As we maneuvered through the aisles, I followed my mom, touching all the different bolts of fabric, especially drawn to the big, giant rolls of fuzzy material used for making stuffed animals. As we finished our shopping and were on our way to the cash registers at the front of the store, something caught my eye. There they sat, thousands of spools of thread. An entire aisle filled with every imaginable color, all perfectly situated in rainbow-like arrangement on either side of me. It was so beautiful and so compelling; in an instant I decided that I must do a little shopping of my own. I quickly gathered spools of thread in my little chubby hands and stuffed them in the pockets of my Toughskins jeans until my pockets bulged and would hold no more. When I was through shopping, I went to the register and joined my mom, who was just about finished checking out.

I don't remember the exact reason

HAVE YOU EVER STOLEN ANYTHING?

_____

_____

_____

_____

_____

I didn't tell my mom that I had just "shopped" my pockets full of thread, but I didn't. On the way home, I sat in the backseat of our big white car, all buckled up, and one by one, quietly pulled out each spool of thread, looking at, admiring, and touching each individual color, then placed it back in my pocket and fished out another spool to look at. When we arrived home, my mother set about unloading all her purchases from the shopping bags, and I decided that now was the time to show her what I had gotten at the store. As I started to fish all the spools of thread from my pockets and line them neatly on the kitchen table, my mother's jaw dropped open and she said something to the effect of, "Honey, you can't do that! That's stealing!" The next thing I remember, we were back in the car and on our way to the store to return the stolen goods. Through tears and sobs, I confessed my crime to the nice lady at the store. I remember that she smiled at me an awful lot. Looking back, that lady may have found my predicament cute or funny, but not me. That was the day I learned about stealing.

NO BIG DEAL

But you might be thinking to yourself, *That's not a big deal at all—a cute little kid taking a few dollars' worth of thread . . .* True, I may have taken only a few dollars' worth of thread from a small fabric store, but the problem with stealing is that it *always* has far-reaching consequences. Let's use my example. If Mom hadn't made me return my ill-gotten loot, what would have happened? First, the store's inventory would not have equaled the money they received from all the purchases. To keep their business running efficiently, they would have to pay for the stolen items somehow. In most instances, a store will offset their losses from theft by raising the prices on their merchandise to make up the difference. Who ends up paying for those higher prices? Every one of their customers. So, in effect, I wasn't just stealing thread, I was taking money from a large number of people's pockets, money that those people could use to feed and clothe their families. No one rightly wants to take food out of a baby's mouth, do they? That starts to sound less appealing, doesn't it? Stealing upsets the economic balance of all society. It is an injustice.

DO YOU THINK NAPSTER SHOULD BE ILLEGAL?

_____

_____

_____

Let me use an example that might hit just a little closer to home. I currently work in the Christian music industry. I have worked with a lot of great artists, like dcTalk, Rebecca St. James, Audio Adrenaline, Toby Mac, Tait, Geoff Moore, Pax217, Stacie Orrico, and many others. My job is to help these artists go into a recording studio and make music for people to listen to. All these artists, myself, and the rest of my coworkers are able to provide food, clothing, and shelter for our families when people purchase the music we make.

But there is a problem. A lot of people (tens of millions of people, in fact) have found a way to "share" their music over the Internet by using file-swapping services instead of going into a store and actually buying a record. Is it a fast and convenient way to hear and get new music? Certainly. But is it stealing? Most definitely. I'm sure that some people would like to argue this point with me, but the government of the United States and nearly all the countries of the world (minus a few notable exceptions) have laws that protect the intellectual property rights of musicians and composers, making this type of activity illegal.

What is more surprising is that either people don't know that getting music without paying for it is stealing or they just don't care. To give you an example, Mark Stuart, lead singer for Audio Adrenaline, told me recently that during three months while they were on tour, he was approached more than twenty times by people wanting him to autograph an illegally burned CDR. Mark was gracious to those people and actually signed their CDRs, but imagine how it made him feel to know that those very people who loved his band's music had also virtually taken money straight from his pocket.

In addition to the artists themselves, I know many people who have recently lost their jobs because the record companies they worked for could no longer afford to pay their wages. This is due, in large part, to lost revenue from illegal file-swapping over the Internet. It's stealing, and it has a significant negative effect on other people.

So we've looked at spools of thread and CDRs, but what are some other ways that we violate God's rule that forbids us to steal?

STEALING IN BIG WAYS

First, there are the big and obvious instances of stealing. Car theft, home burglary, big-time jewel heists, and stealing top-secret information from the government are all the stuff of TV and movies and make for an interesting story. But there are many other big examples of stealing that aren't quite so obvious. Throughout history, and even today, there are people who will take others against their will and take away their freedom for some evil purpose, through kidnapping and slavery. Let's remember again that God wants to "set the captive free," and these two things are in direct violation of this rule. Most of us, however, will not become jewel thieves or kidnappers, so let's look at some subtler ways that stealing creeps into our lives.

WHAT GIVES THINGS VALUE?

_____

_____

_____

STEALING IN SMALL WAYS

Stealing always involves some level of untruthfulness, unfairness, and greed, which are qualities that have the tendency to sneak up on us. Let's say you just received a new Sony PlayStation 2 gaming system from your parents for Christmas, and now you want to get rid of your older PlayStation 1. You decide to sell it to someone in your third-period English class whom you don't know very well, but you overheard that person saying he was looking to buy a used PlayStation 1. You don't have any idea what to charge him for it, so you log on to eBay to see what they are selling for. The game console and two dual shock controllers in used but mint condition are selling for sixty bucks. You tell your classmate you are willing to sell your gaming system to him "as is" for sixty dollars because that is what they go for on eBay. He accepts your offer and the deal is done. Now you have money in your pocket to run out and buy another game. The thing that you chose not to tell the buyer is that one of the controller buttons has an intermittent short in it and doesn't always work very well. Was that a fair transaction? Was that stealing? By choosing to be greedy, and choosing not to be fully truthful and fair, you have ended with unrighteous gain—or stealing.

Another way of stealing involves obtaining anything at the unfair expense of others. For instance, one of the job responsibilities your parents gave you is to mow the yard every week. In exchange for your work, your parents give you twenty dollars each time you mow the yard. Midway through the summer, and after a particularly hot afternoon of mowing the lawn, you are sitting in the shade with a big tall glass of cold lemonade, thinking about how wiped out you feel and how much you hate to mow the yard . . . and then it hits you! Why not hire your younger brother to mow the lawn for you but only pay him five dollars? You know that he gets that much for trimming the sidewalks and driveway after you mow, and you bet he sure would like the extra money. This way you wouldn't have to do *any* work, and you'd still get fifteen bucks because you are such a generous sibling. And even better, you will have all your afternoons free to hang out with the rest of your friends at the pool.

IS YOUR WORK HONEST?

Is this the same as stealing, or are you just a shrewd businessperson? That's a very good question, but it is one you must answer for yourself. Jeremiah 22:13–17 cautions against building up our own riches by cheating others or treating them unfairly. The Bible also gives an ominous warning about how we treat our work and those who work for us. Colossians 3:23–4:1 says,

> In all the work you are doing, work the best you can. Work as if you were doing it for the Lord, not for people. Remember that you will receive your reward from the Lord, which he promised to his people. You are serving the Lord Christ. But remember that anyone who does wrong will be punished for that wrong, and the Lord treats everyone the same. Masters, give what is good and fair to your slaves. Remember that you have a Master in heaven.

Basically, this passage is saying that in matters of work and employment, we are to be fair. This applies to both the boss and the worker. The worker should work hard, not only to please the boss but to please the Lord as well, because both will reward them. And in the case where we might be the employer or the boss, God is telling us to provide our workers with what is right and fair and to treat them well. Even though we may be boss here on earth, we work for God, the Boss of the entire earth and heaven.

There are so many other ways in which we steal. Borrowing something from a friend and neglecting to return it, looking at answers from your neighbor's test in order get a good grade, or "sharing" your employee discount at J. Crew with the entire cheerleading squad are just a few more examples. There are big things and small things, physical things and spiritual things that can be stolen from others by us.

HEART CONDITION

When we find ourselves breaking this rule of God's, what does that say about our hearts? It tells us that we just aren't satisfied with what God has given us, even though God has given us a lot. It also reveals that we really don't trust God to give us what we need and that we think we should take matters into our own hands.

Jesus tells us several important things that let us know where our hearts should be. First, in Matthew 6:19–21, He says that we are not to store up treasures for ourselves here on earth, because "your heart will be where your treasure is." Jesus also tells us not to worry about food or clothes, because God knows our needs and takes care of His creation. He says, "The thing you should want most is God's kingdom and doing what God wants. Then all these other things you need will be given to you" (Matthew 6:33). Finally, Jesus reminds us that we should ask God for what we need, and He will be very generous. He says, "Even though you are bad, you know how to give good gifts to your children. How much more your heavenly Father will give good things to those who ask him!" (Matthew 7:11).

ARE YOU SATISFIED WITH WHAT GOD HAS GIVEN YOU?

LIVING IT OUT

So how should we live in light of rule eight? We know that we should *not* steal and that we should focus on God's kingdom and doing what He wants: He will take care of our needs. Here's another thought: Instead of taking from someone what doesn't belong to you, why not give what does belong to you to someone else? Throughout the Bible, God's people are encouraged to be generous. In Deuteronomy 15:7, 10, God instructs Israel, "If there are poor among you, in one of the towns of the land the LORD your God is giving you, do not be selfish or greedy toward them. . . . Give freely to the poor person, and do not wish that you didn't have to give. The LORD your God will bless your work and everything you touch." Proverbs 11:25 says, "Whoever gives to others will get richer; those who help others will themselves be helped." And again, in Proverbs 22:9 we find, "Generous people will be blessed, because they share their food with the poor."

CONCLUSION

May the love of God be illustrated in our lives as instructed by 1 John 3:17–18:

> Suppose someone has enough to live and sees a brother or sister in need, but does not help. Then God's love is not living in that person. My children, we should love people not only with words and talk, but by our actions and true caring.

FIVE THINGS I'LL DO TO STEAL LESS AND GIVE MORE ARE:

1.
2.
3.
4.
5.

LIE

LIAR, LIAR

RULE #9

You shall not bear false witness against your neighbor.
(EXODUS 20:16, NKJV)

he tongue is a deadly thing and can start a big fire. James 3:2–10 says,

> We all make many mistakes. If people never said anything wrong, they would be perfect and able to control their entire selves, too. When we put bits into the mouths of horses to make them obey us, we can control their whole bodies. Also a ship is very big, and it is pushed by strong winds. But a very small rudder controls that big ship, making it go wherever the pilot wants. It is the same with the tongue. It is a small part of the body, but it brags about great things.
>
> A big forest fire can be started with only a little flame. And the tongue is like a fire. It is a whole world of evil among the parts of our bodies. The tongue spreads its evil through the whole body. The tongue is set on fire by hell, and it starts a fire that influences all of life. People can tame every kind of wild animal, bird, reptile, and fish, and they have tamed them, but no one can tame the tongue. It is wild and evil and full of deadly poison. We use our tongues to praise our Lord and Father, but then we curse people, whom God made like himself. Praises and curses come from the same mouth! My brothers and sisters, this should not happen.

Again, we have a rule that has to do with our mouths and what comes out of them. This must be of great importance to God, and it is important here on earth as well. In chapter 3, we looked at how God expects us to treat His name and how we are to honor Him when we speak of Him to others. The ninth commandment has to do with how we speak about our fellowman.

With this rule, the obvious idea is that we are not to lie about or against our neighbor. This falls right in line with the previous four rules on how we are to treat others. The language in the New King James Version leads us to think in terms of a courtroom setting, where a person's reputation and future hang in the balance. It is here that we can observe how our words, whether true or false, have great consequence to the lives of other people.

HOW HAS A LIE HURT YOU IN THE PAST?

MALICIOUS LIES

Fourth period is your biology class during your sophomore year in high school. You have always been curious about the way things work and have discovered that the subject of biology and the way God created things to function is quite fascinating. Your teacher also has an evident love for the subject and keeps the class excited and interested to learn more. The best part is that you are pulling an A in the class, and next semester you will make the honor roll for the very first time. The only drawback to the whole class is that your assigned seat is right in front of the class clown. We'll call him Hunter. He is quite obnoxious, always messing around in class, and he is often a big-time distraction.

Christmas break is only a few days away, and you are just putting the finishing touches on your end-of-semester exam (for which you have studied your brains out) when your teacher asks you to stay a few moments after class. At that point, your teacher tells you that she thinks she saw Hunter copying answers from your test, but she is not certain, and she wants to know if you noticed it too. You were so intent on taking the test that you wouldn't have noticed a zebra wearing a party hat and dancing through the room, and you have no earthly idea if the class clown was copying answers from your paper—but wait . . . the school policy is that anyone caught cheating will be permanently kicked out of the class; they will automatically fail and have to retake the course next year. Wouldn't it be great not to have all that constant clowning and distraction caused by Hunter next semester? You really don't like him very much, and it sure would make it easier to concentrate if *he* weren't sitting behind you. Here is where you have a choice. How do you respond to your teacher?

WHEN HAVE YOU EVER "STRETCHED THE TRUTH" JUST A BIT?

1. *I was too engrossed with my test and didn't notice a thing. Sorry, but I have no idea if someone was cheating off me.* Maybe he was cheating off your test; maybe he was not. You choose to tell the truth completely and leave the fate of Hunter in the hands

of the teacher and what the teacher observed. You give an honest answer.

2. *Well, Hunter is a goof-off, after all, and he probably didn't study very well for this test. It sounds like something he might do.* You have found what appears to be a loophole! You don't necessarily tell a lie, but you don't necessarily tell the truth either. By replying in this way, you are helping to create or reaffirm suspicion about Hunter in the teacher's mind. You are calling his character into question. You have dodged the question, but by doing so, you will have rid yourself of Hunter in your favorite class next semester.

3. *I didn't want to say anything, but I'm pretty certain he was cheating off my test, and I'm so glad you noticed it too.* Whew! No more Hunter next semester! Surely your teacher saw him cheating, and even though you don't know this for sure, you're just telling the teacher what she wants to hear anyway. One small lie is all it took to be rid of this loud-mouthed pest. Now you can learn biology in peace next semester, without the constant disruption. Your grades will certainly get even better. Who knows, maybe you'll even land a great scholarship to your preferred college! You told a lie, but so what? No one will ever know.

Think of the far-reaching consequences to Hunter in this situation. Even though he is a pest, this could potentially be the tipping point that causes him not to graduate on time, get pegged as a cheater, drop out of school, or any number of bad things that could hurt him and his future. The words that come out of our mouths are more powerful than we can imagine; words, once spoken, have the ability to grow and snowball out of our control. Once a thing is said, it can never be fully retrieved. Again, we should not give false testimony against (wrongly accuse) others to get them in any kind of trouble. Not being fully truthful can have very damaging effects on someone's reputation. God wants us to look out for others and take care of others with our words. That is what this rule is all about. God makes it clear that being truthful about others is the right thing to do. Always. Don't tell lies. But that isn't always so easy or simple, is it?

We've looked at the most obvious form of lying, something that we will call Malicious Lies. But there are other kinds of lies that require our attention, though their effect on others is a little less black-and-white. Let's examine some other types of "lies" that at first glance don't appear to be so hurtful.

IS JOKING AROUND WITH SOMEONE ACTUALLY LYING?

PLAYFUL LIES

Here's one that has been played on me more than once. I can remember several instances when a good friend of mine and I were hanging out in a public place and he would lean close and whisper in my ear, "Hey, Mark! X Y Z!" (i.e., eXamine Your Zipper). There's hardly anything more embarrassing than realizing that your fly is down in a public place. After he would say those fateful words, I would flush bright red and as quickly as I could without seeming obvious, I would discreetly make sure I was zipped up—which, of course, I was. My friend would then double over in laughter as I realized that I had once again been played. He was just joking around. And it was funny—to both of us. Just a funny little joke between friends, right? But it was also by definition a lie. What about that?

What about when a friend or acquaintance starts to tell a tall tale or a story that exaggerates the truth for the amusement of all who are listening? ("The other day I was riding my bike up this hill in my neighborhood that's like ninety miles long; I was passed by this super-skinny girl on a skateboard who weighed like fifteen pounds. . . .") The listener usually knows from the beginning that the storyteller is only being overly descriptive and doesn't mean to be deceptive, but simply wants to make the story even more expressive and colorful. It's not technically the literal truth, but it sure makes for a more interesting story. Is that wrong?

IS FALSE FLATTERY A LIE?

Is it acceptable to lie for the sole purpose of bringing some laughter and joy into an otherwise dull day? Good laughter and storytelling are part of all our lives and bring us great joy, but here is where we have to be careful once again. Proverbs 26:18–19 says, "Like a madman shooting deadly, burning arrows is the one who tricks a neighbor and then says, 'I was just joking.'" There is a fine line here to be wary of. Telling untruths for the purpose of humor or storytelling can easily backfire, because one cannot always control the effects the jokes or stories will have on the listeners. The point at which the listener is deceived or ridiculed is where the rule has been broken. It is always best to weigh our words carefully and think of what reaction we might cause when we speak.

WHITE LIES

Another form of truth/nontruth that deserves a quick look is the Courteous Lie. Are there times when, for the sake of being polite, you will say something you don't exactly mean? If you are invited to someone's house for a meal and the food that has been served to you tastes funny or is burned, and they ask, "How do you like your meal?" do you tell your host the food is rotten? You don't unless you are a mean and cold-hearted person. No, I would expect that you or I would swallow hard and tell them everything tastes fine and we would continue to pretend to enjoy the meal. This is what is commonly referred to as a "white lie."

So how did we do in that situation? Yes, we were polite; we chose not to say something that would hurt or offend our gracious host, but we didn't exactly tell the truth. Wrong or right? Being polite is not meant to be a graceful way of being dishonest. Politeness is a way in which we honor and respect others. In other words, being polite is a way for us to show love to another. There is no need for you to communicate your negative thoughts to someone; that is not what honesty is all about.

Let's look at what God's Word tells us in 1 Corinthians 13:5–7 about love and how we are to love others:

> Love is not rude, is not selfish, and does not get upset with others. Love does not count up wrongs that have been done. Love is not happy with evil but is happy with the truth. Love patiently accepts all things. It always trusts, always hopes, and always remains strong.

Hmmm, love is not rude. So we probably should *not* tell our host that their food is unappetizing. But love is happy with the truth. Now we're back where we started, right? Well, love also patiently endures all things. So what should the answer to our host be? If you or I were to stop, think, and consider what we were to say, we would find a way to answer them in kindness and sincerity that honors, respects, and loves that person. "Thank you for your generosity in having me over for dinner. I really appreciate all the hard work you put into preparing this meal. This has been a real blessing to me!"

There are a great number of other uses of our tongues that don't show love for our fellowman and break this rule. Think about how often you or your friends spread rumors or gossip, with information that may or may not be true. What about scoffing, bragging, or flattery? Anytime we speak of others and it is not to their benefit, we do wrong—wrong by that person and wrong by God.

WHAT IS A PRACTICAL WAY TO SHOW LOVE TO OTHERS THROUGH YOUR SPEECH?

_____

_____

_____

_____

CONCLUSION

With so many ways not to speak, sometimes you might think it best not to say anything, ever. But that is not the case. God gave us the gift of speech and communication for good reasons. Just as speaking lies or hurtful words can be harmful to others, speaking good and truthful words can be very beneficial to others.

If someone is down or discouraged, we have the ability to pick them up and encourage them with a kind word. Proverbs 12:25 says, "Worry is a heavy load, but a kind word cheers you up." If someone doesn't know the truth, we have the ability to tell him or her the good story of Jesus. With our mouths we can say we are thankful, or we can offer forgiveness.

God gave us the ability to bless others, to serve others, to rejoice in good things, to defend the innocent, and to speak out for justice. We are called to love others by building them up with encouragement. Don't be afraid to speak, but remember to speak what is true, honest, beautiful, and all that is good news.

As God tells us in Ephesians 4:29, "When you talk, do not say harmful things, but say what people need—words that will help others become stronger. Then what you say will do good to those who listen to you."

FIVE WAYS I WILL IMPROVE MY SPEECH ARE:

1.

2.

3.

4.

5.

I NEED THIS

MATERIAL GIRL (OR BOY)

You shall not covet your neighbor's house; you shall not covet your neighbor's wife, nor his male servant, nor his female servant, nor his ox, nor his donkey, nor anything that is your neighbor's.

(EXODUS 20:17, NKJV)

Taken at face value, the previous rules pertain to our exterior selves—how we act or speak. However, as we've discussed with all of them, these rules also relate to our interior selves. For example, with adultery and murder, Jesus specifically addresses the fact that the conditions of our hearts and minds are just as important as our physical actions.

With the tenth commandment, we have a rule that explicitly talks about our desires. You must not *want* things that belong to your neighbor. Many translations use the word *covet*, which means "to desire wrongfully or to wish for excessively."

DANGEROUS DESIRE

On a practical level, there are very good reasons that God tells us we are not even to want to have things that belong to another person. For one thing, thinking and wanting very well might lead to doing. Once our minds begin ruminating on a desire, it can sometimes be very hard to let it go unsatisfied. I'll give you a relatively harmless example. Let's say that it is a sweltering hot summer day and you run into a friend at the mall. As you're talking about what you've been up to that day, she tells you she just tried the new summer ice-cream flavor at the shop down the street, and it was really good. As you move on to the CD store, you think about that ice cream your friend was talking about. It sure sounded good, and it *is* such a miserably hot day outside. As you flip through the racks, it keeps coming to your mind— the caramel, the fudge stripes, the peanut butter cups. Cold and tasty. Even though dinner is only two hours away, you just can't get that ice cream out of your mind. So, on your way home, you stop in and order yourself a sugar cone with two scoops. Now, this is a fairly minor instance of desire leading to action, but we all know that our wants can move us to make much more serious and often destructive choices.

DO MAGAZINES CAUSE YOU TO COVET?

Stealing and adultery both begin with wanting something or someone that is not ours. Let's look at a few Bible verses that bear this out. In the book of Joshua, chapter 7, God becomes very angry at the Israelites because one of them is keeping things that God had commanded be destroyed. In verses 20 and 21, the guilty man, Achan, admits, "It is true! I have sinned against the LORD, the God of Israel. This is what I did: Among the things I saw was a beautiful coat from Babylonia and about five pounds of silver and more than one and one-fourth pounds of gold. I wanted these things very much for myself, so I took them. You will find them buried in the ground under my tent, with the silver underneath." Micah 2:1–2 talks about people "who plan wickedness, who lie on their beds and make evil plans. When the morning light comes, they do what they planned, because they have the power to do so. They want fields, so they take them; they want houses, so they take them away. They cheat people to get their houses; they rob them even of their property." Desire can lead to planning, and then to action.

Even if people who covet don't actually try to get what they want, it can still affect the lives of those around them, as well as the coveters themselves. The internal tension and unrest that come with coveting will likely be evident in their lives. Have you ever consciously or unconsciously changed your behavior toward a friend after you found out they got something you both had been wanting?

Let's say there's a new guy at your school. You know that all the girls, including your girlfriend of six months, think he's really cute. If your girlfriend has more than a passing interest in this guy, you'll probably know, even if she doesn't actually cheat on you. As her thoughts are consumed with the new guy, you might see changes in her behavior, like calling you less or not paying as much attention when you're talking. Now let's transfer that scenario to a marriage relationship. If you're a man who has thoughts of being with your friend's wife, not only will it affect your relationship with your wife, it will also cause negative changes in your attitude toward your friend.

WHAT HAPPENS TO YOU WHEN YOU WANT SOMETHING YOU DON'T HAVE?

_____

_____

_____

_____

MORE! MORE!

We've talked a lot about how these rules demonstrate God's love for us and how they lead to freedom. We can see that coveting leads to tension and unrest, both internally and in our relationships with others. Coveting enslaves us, plain and simple. God does not want that for us. He wants the lives of His children to be full of peace and love. It is because He wants the best for us that He instructs us not to covet our neighbor's spouse or belongings.

As you know, it can be very difficult not to fixate on what is not ours. Looking back to Adam and Eve, we see it has been this way since the beginning of sin. You'll remember that God had given Adam and Eve permission to eat fruit from all the trees in the Garden of Eden, except the Tree of the Knowledge of Good and Evil, as that would lead to death. One day the snake came to Eve and told her that God's warning about the tree was not true. If they ate from that tree, the snake said, they would learn about good and evil and be like God. Eve was tempted by the ability to be like God, which is a possibility that belonged solely to God. Adam and Eve wanted something that belonged to Someone else. And we all know what happened when they ate that fruit.

Now, there's a key point in the story of Adam and Eve. Genesis 1:28–29 says, "God blessed them and said, 'Have many children and grow in number. Fill the earth and be its master. Rule over the fish in the sea and over the birds in the sky and over every living thing that moves on the earth.' God said, 'Look, I have given you all the plants that have grain for seeds and all the trees whose fruits have seeds in them. They will be food for you.'" And in Genesis 2:16–17a, we read, "The LORD God commanded him, 'You may eat the fruit from any tree in the garden, but you must not eat the fruit from the tree which gives the knowledge of good and evil.'" What do we see in these passages? We see that God had given Adam and Eve a lot. He gave them His blessing, dominion over the animals, plenty of food to eat, and companionship in each other, as well as the ability to procreate. And what was Adam and Eve's response to all of these gifts? They wanted more. Wow! Does this sound like anyone you know? I would imagine you're noticing that most of us bear a striking resemblance to Adam and Eve in this way. I believe this is another reason God gives us this rule. When we focus on things that we want, we tend to forget all that we do have.

Let's look at one more story that should bring all these ideas together. If you have a younger sibling or cousin, or even if you've ever gone to the grocery store, you're no doubt familiar with the temper tantrum. Well, for the purpose of this story, let's say you've volunteered to help out in the Sunday school class for three-year-olds at your church. There are about twelve kids in the room, including a boy named Parker and a girl named Tori. While the two teachers are at the table popping out the perforated illustrations to use on the flannelboard, you're keeping an eye on the kids playing in the part of the room with all the toys.

WHAT DOES A TEMPER TANTRUM LOOK LIKE FOR YOU?

_____

_____

_____

_____

As Parker is working on a Lego rocket ship, he sees Tori walking around with a stuffed lamb puppet on her hand. You watch as Parker gets up and snatches the puppet off Tori's hand. With a look of surprise on her face, Tori starts to sniffle. You walk over to Parker and explain that Tori was playing with the lamb and ask him to give it back to her. He doesn't obey, so you take it from him and give it back to Tori. Now what happens? Parker throws a tantrum. He screams, "But I want it!" over and over, and his eyes well up with tears. Pretty soon he's crying so hard he can hardly breathe. You try to calm him down and point out some other stuffed animals in the room that are sitting on shelves. Each time he is able to catch a breath, he tells you again, "But I wanted to play with that one."

Now let's look at the thoughts and feelings of all the characters involved here. Parker, for one, in his obsession with getting what he wants (something that "belongs" to someone else), is making himself miserable. Tori, on the other hand, is a little hurt and scared. It's hard for her to enjoy the puppet in peace, as she's now afraid that Parker will come and grab it from her again. What about the other kids in the room? Well, this was certainly a disruptive ordeal that added tension to their playtime. And finally, how does Parker's action and reaction look to you and the other adults in the room? Ridiculous. You can see that there's a room full of great toys available for play. You are also kind of upset about the effect he's had on the other kids, as well as on himself. And where did all this start? It started with desire and covetousness in one little boy's heart. Unfortunately, there are many times when we are not unlike that three-year-old. And honestly, it's pretty easy to find ourselves seeking things that do not belong to us. This rule exposes our hearts and shows us how far off we are from where we should be.

GOOD DESIRES

I'd like to take a minute to clarify something, just in case there is any confusion. This rule does not mean that we are to be completely devoid of any wants or desires. After all, that's part of what makes us human beings and individuals. For example, we want to eat and sleep because that's how God made us. Your desire to paint or cook or write or build things might let you know what God wants you to be doing here on earth, either as a profession or simply as a hobby to enjoy. And you will probably find your husband or wife because of an attraction to them and a desire for companionship.

So how are we supposed to live in light of this rule? For one thing, we should be thankful. Psalm 100:4–5 says, "Come into his city with songs of thanksgiving and into his courtyards with songs of praise. Thank him and praise his name. The LORD is good. His love is forever, and his loyalty goes on and on." In our thanksgiving, we acknowledge that God is the One who takes care of our needs and wants. We are also instructed to ask God to supply our needs and to set our desires before Him. Ephesians 6:18 advises, "Pray in the Spirit at all times with all kinds of prayers, asking for everything you need. To do this you must always be ready and never give up. Always pray for all God's people." As we pray, we are also to trust that He will continue to give us what is best for us.

> **LIST SOME OF THE GOOD DESIRES YOU HAVE.**

CONCLUSION

We'll close by looking at what Jesus has to say about our needs and wants. In Luke 12:29–31, Jesus says, "Don't always think about what you will eat or what you will drink, and don't keep worrying. All the people in the world are trying to get these things, and your Father knows you need them. But seek God's kingdom, and all the other things you need will be given to you." To add more clarity and emphasis, let's also read Jesus' words from Matthew 6:33: "The thing you should want most is God's kingdom and doing what God wants. Then all these other things you need will be given to you." Let's ask God to work in our hearts so that our wants are in line with His, and thank Him for taking care of our needs.

"Enjoy serving the LORD, and he will give you what you want" (Psalm 37:4).

FIVE WAYS I WILL CHANGE PATTERNS OF COVETING IN MY LIFE ARE:

1. _____

2. _____

3. _____

4. _____

5. _____

SUMMING UP

CHAPTER # 11

We have come to the end of our list of rules, so let's look back at what we've learned. We know that in all we do, we must love God and put Him first above everything else. In our love toward God, we must not bow to or worship anything but the one true God, and we must respect Him in the way we speak of Him. We have also learned that God has set aside a day each week for us to worship Him and, in the process, be restored and refreshed by Him. Our rules tell us to honor our parents, guardians, and all in authority over us, and to respect all life and work to protect it. We must keep ourselves sexually pure and help to protect that purity in others. We shouldn't steal from others but be generous with what we have, and we should also keep from telling lies, using our words instead to build others up. And finally, we should not long for things we don't have but be thankful and content with all that the Lord has provided us.

All these rules tie together into God's perfect plan for how we should live. Jesus said it best in Matthew 22:37–40:

> "Love the Lord your God with all your heart, all your soul, and all your mind." This is the first and most important command. And the second command is like the first: "Love your neighbor as you love yourself." All the law and the writings of the prophets depend on these two commands.

The rules are so very well summed up by Jesus in love. Love is not just an inward thing; true love reveals itself in an outpouring. An outpouring toward God, who He is and what He has done for us, and toward our neighbor—our fellow human, our literal neighbors, friends, family, and especially those brothers and sisters in the family of God. Christians should be the number one recipients of God's love through us, as we are called to be in fellowship and accountability with them and because we know that God's ultimate sacrifice was paid for them as well. If every single one of us were to follow these rules, we would live in a perfect world. So . . . how well do you do following all these rules? Not so good? Me neither.

If you want to know the truth, these rules do three things. First, they show us how perfect and good God really is. Second, they tell us how we should live. Third, because not one of us has ever been able to live by these rules all the time, they show us how wicked and self-centered our hearts really are. They reveal to us how badly we need help. But God doesn't leave us hanging out there all alone in our sinfulness and brokenness. "I look up to the hills, but where does my help come from? My help comes from the LORD, who made heaven and earth. He will not let you be defeated. He who guards you never sleeps" (Psalm 121:1–3). That's right. Our help comes from the Lord. And how thankful we should be! If it were up to us, we would surely make quite a mess of things. But God sent Jesus to free us—free us from sin that tells us we are the most important, because we aren't. Our rules make us free to give of ourselves to God and to others. We are free to be rebels in this world and to live radical, world-changing lives. We are free to love God fully; we are free to love others wholly. Do you want to live a life that matters? Lean into these rules and be free.

BIBLIOGRAPHY

The following authors and their works helped to better frame my understanding of the Ten Commandments. They were all a great source of inspiration in the writing of this book.

Barnum, Mary. "Old Testament Understanding for the Names of God." *Xenos Christian Fellowship: The Crossroads Project Online Journal* 2 (n.d.). Online: http:// www.xenos.org/ministries/crossroads/ OnlineJournal/issue2/nmsofgod.htm

Calvin, John. *Institutes of the Christian Religion*. Translated by Ford Lewis Battles. Philadelphia: Westminster Press, 1960.

Douma, Jochem. *The Ten Commandments: Manual for the Christian Life*. Translated by Nelson D. Kloosterman. Phillipsburg, NJ: P&R Publishing, 1996.

Green, Jay P., Sr., ed. and trans. *The Interlinear Bible: Hebrew—Greek—English*. Peabody, MA: Hendrickson Publishers, 1976, 1986.

Henry, Matthew. *Matthew Henry's Commentary on the Whole Bible*. Nashville: Thomas Nelson, Inc., 1997.

Hoekema, Anthony A. *Created in God's Image*. Grand Rapids: Eerdmanns, 1986.

Jones, David Clyde. *Biblical Christian Ethics*. Grand Rapids: Baker Books, 1994.

Strong, James. *Strong's Exhaustive Concordance of the Bible*. Nashville: Thomas Nelson, 1990.

Unger, Merrill F. *Unger's Bible Dictionary*. Chicago: Moody Press, 1957, 1975.

The Westminster Confession of Faith. Published by the Presbyterian Church in America Committee for Christian Education & Publications, Atlanta, GA, 1990.

SUPPORT THE DATA AGENDA

We at Transit support the work of the DATA (Debt, AIDS, Trade, Africa) organization in Africa. Every day more than 5,500 people in Africa die from the AIDS virus. And every day more than 1,700 children are infected with HIV. Six times more girls than boys are infected. We cannot stand by while this holocaust happens before our eyes without doing anything to help. This is the moment in history when we face our humanity, our faith, and our commitment to God. We are commanded to love our neighbor. Africa is our neighbor. Will you help?

Write a letter to the president, your senators, and your congressmen today! You could change the world.

Log on to **www.datadata.org** today!

CHECK OUT THESE OTHER TRANSIT BOOKS!

Witnessing 101
What to say to your friends
when words fail you.
By Tim Baker
$10.99

Mission: Africa
Take a vacation from everything
you take for granted.
$11.99

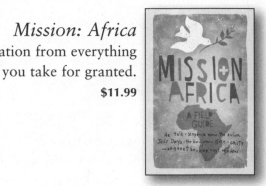

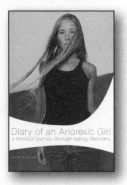

Diary of an Anorexic Girl
The based-on-a-true-story account
of one girl's battle with anorexia.
By Morgan Menzie
$12.99

Revolve
The complete New Testament designed
like a fashion magazine for girls!
$14.99